Vladimir Soloviev

A Russian Newman

VLADIMIR SOLOVIEV

AT THE AGE OF 38

VLADIMIR SOLOVIEV

A RUSSIAN NEWMAN

(1853–1900)

BY

MICHEL D'HERBIGNY

TRANSLATED BY

A. M. BUCHANAN, M.A.

Semantron

San Rafael, Ca

Second, facsimile edition
Semantron, 2007
First edition, R. & T Washbourne, Ltd., 1918

For information, address:
Semantron, P.O. Box 151011
San Rafael, California 94915, USA

Library of Congress Cataloging-in-Publication Data

Herbigny, Michel d', 1880–1957.
Vladimir Soloviev: a Russian Newman: (1853–1900)/
Michel D'Herbigny; translated by A.M. Buchanan. — Reprint ed.

p. cm.
Originally published: London: R.&T. Washbourne, 1918.
ISBN-13: 978-1-59731-251-6 (pbk.: alk. paper)
ISBN-13: 978-1-59731-276-9 (hardcover: alk. paper)
1. Solovyov, Vladimir Sergeyevich, 1853–1900. I. Title.
B4267.H47 2007
197—dc22   2007027057

CONTENTS

7

VLADIMIR SOLOVIEV
THE RUSSIAN NEWMAN

INTRODUCTION*

ONE of the fortunes of war has been the revelation
to Western eyes of a Russian mystic. It is Vladimir
Soloviev. He is not only the foremost spiritual
philosopher of Russia, but he is also one of the most
distinguished types of the modern mind. Towards
the end of his life he happened to write a book
against Tolstoï, combating that writer's doctrine of
the non-resistance of evil. The book has lately received two translations into English, as a statement
of the philosophy of war from the Russian point
of view.

The subject of war, however, holds but a secondary
place in the book, and indeed a very secondary place
in the life of Soloviev. His great lifework was an
exposition and propaganda of the claims of the
Universal Church. He was a convert from Orthodoxy to Catholicism, and the one ruling passion
of his life was to familiarize Russia with the idea of
a Universal Church, monarchical in its constitution.
This is the chief reason for calling him the Russian

* Article on Soloviev, contributed to the *Catholic World* by
Father Thomas Gerrard.

I

Newman. There were other striking similarities between the two men, although their divergencies were even more striking and more numerous.

Soloviev, like Newman, was very lonely in his soul. He worked always from within—the voice of conscience was his all-impelling guide and force. His method was the personal one. He conceived in his own peculiar way a philosophy of the whole man, which was neither intellectualist, voluntarist, nor sentimentalist. With the watchword of " integralism," he stood for the due equipoise of all the faculties of man in the search for truth. He worked out for himself a method remarkably analogous to Newman's doctrine of the Illative Sense, but with this important difference, that he always preserved a profound respect for the use and the value of the syllogism.

Yet if, on the one hand, he was personal and subjective, it was always with a sane appreciation of the value of objective evidence. Like Newman again, he took a special delight in the study of Holy Scripture and the Fathers, of Church history and the development of religion. Like Newman, too, he had an ardent love for his own country. He thought of Catholicism for Russia, and believed that if only Russia were Catholic it would mean the religious transformation of the whole world.

Unlike Newman, Soloviev never became a priest. Both before and after his conversion he preferred to work as a layman. Nevertheless, he deemed that he could best follow his calling by remaining a celibate. Once, at the age of eighteen, he did think of marriage, but, by the time he had arrived at the age of twenty, he had fully resolved to lead a single life.

Soloviev was born on January 16, 1853, the son of the Russian historian, Serge Mikhaïlovitch Soloviev. His grandfather was a priest of the Orthodox Church, whilst on his mother's side he was related to the philosopher Skovorod. Thus all the influences of his childhood tended to imbue him with the spirit of the Slav. He grew up a Slav of the Slavs. What he wrote of his father in later years was a summary of the influences which bore on his own early life: " With a most passionate love he loved Orthodoxy, science, and the Russian fatherland."

The son, however, did not remain long under the supervision of his parents. In 1864, at the age of eleven, he passed into the gymnasium at Moscow. At once, even in these boyish years, he began to show himself alive to the thought of the West. It was something other than what he had been accustomed to in his parental home. He read Strauss's *Leben Jesu* and Renan's *Vie de Jésus*. But the book that most captivated him was Büchner's *Force and Matter*. It had just been censured, and was consequently in the hands of many of the older students. And consequently, also, it had to be in the hands of this boy philosopher. He read each book in its original language, and persuaded himself that he was solving a great question. So at the age of fourteen he came to the conclusion that he could never more take part in any religious act.

According to his judgment the Christian faith could not withstand the discoveries of science. The spiritual world was an illusion.

Such ill-digested food, however, could never agree with him. Both his mind and his feelings were dissatisfied with his immature conclusion. In later years he wrote of this time: " At the age of thirteen or fourteen, when I was a zealous materialist my great problem was this: How can any sensible people remain Christians ?   And I could only explain the strange fact by supposing either hypocrisy or a peculiar kind of madness.   This was silly enough for a boy. . . ."

It was his father who saved him.   He took him seriously and impressed upon him the importance of the problem of life.   Young Soloviev continued to treat his problem seriously, and for three years remained absorbed in the obscurities of matter and evil.   His very sincerity served him well and kept him straight morally.   Where his fellow-students carried the subversive doctrines to a practical conclusion, Soloviev kept true to his saner instincts. In fact it was through one of his rationalist authors that he found his conversion, the one being none other than Spinoza.   Through the study of that writer he gradually reached a conviction of the reality of the spirit world, and of the necessary existence of God.   Of course, there was in Spinoza the danger of the other extreme.   The reaction from materialism might easily, under such a leader, have led him into an equally crude spiritualism. But Soloviev saw farther than his master.   His

own personal method of philosophizing made him
see that God must be both personal and transcendent.
On leaving the gymnasium he had decided to be a
philosopher by profession, but not for the sake of a
living, nor yet for the sake of philosophy. He had
a particular detestation of the principle of art for
art's sake. All these things were for the sake of
love—love of God and love of souls. Hence he
could have no use for the impersonal God of Spinoza.
.Thus did his personal method carry him over the
stumbling-block of pantheism. Having cleared his
own mind, he next sought to bring his conviction
to bear on his country. But he found himself
opposed both on the right and on the left. His
countrymen were divided into two camps, those
who stood for the introduction of liberal thought
from the West, and those who stood for the national
traditions. To these parties were given the names
respectively of Occidentalists and Slavophiles.

The Occidentalists, enamoured of the catchwords
" liberty " and " evolution," were ready for every
kind of revolution. Existing institutions no longer
commanded their respect. They wanted no more
Tsar, nor yet any more Orthodox Church. They
could even do without any form of Christianity
whatsoever. If they were to have any religion at
all, they preferred the positivism of Auguste Comte.

The Slavophiles, on the other hand, were guided
by two simple and almost identical principles,
namely, to have nothing to do with the West, and
never to depart from the customs of the East. This
double principle, of course, included the further one

that Orthodoxy was to remain the religion of Russia, and that every resistance must be offered to the Roman Catholic Church. The offices both in the State and in the Church were naturally filled with Slavophiles, whilst the Universities afforded opportunities for the Occidentalists. Both parties, however, were united in their hostility to Rome.

Such was the general trend of thought when Soloviev entered upon his career as a professor of philosophy. He set for himself the task of reconciling the opposing camps. He would show that liberty and authority were not mutually exclusive, but that an equipoise could be established between them. This equipoise was also to be attained between faith and science—one could be learned without giving up the faith. It was also to be attained between the Church and the fatherland— one could belong to a Universal Church and at the same time be loyal to one's country. Soloviev was thus above all parties, and, consequently, won from them varying measures of approval and opposition. The opposition, especially in the forms of the rigours of censorship, was so insistent throughout his short life that it was not until after his death that his influence began to produce evident effects.

The ground wherein he proposed to sow his seed had been prepared by two other philosophers, to whom he also was much indebted. The sterility of Russian thought had been mercilessly exposed by Pierre Tchadaïev. The evils, economic and political, with which Russia was afflicted, had been laid bare by Leo Tolstoï. But neither Tolstoï nor Tchadaïev provided a remedy. Their work had to be perfected by Soloviev.

Before he had reached the age of twenty he had come back to the Christian faith. The concluding years of his student life at the University of Moscow were marked by a wide variety of interests—he followed the courses of history and philology, physical science and mathematics, and also a course of theology at the ecclesiastical academy.

At length the time came for his final examination, which took place at Petrograd on November 24, 1874. His first thesis, which was formulated against the positivists, was entitled *A Criticism of Western Philosophy*. It treated of the double evolution of thought, idealism from Descartes to Hegel, and empiricism from Bacon to Mill. Both lines of thought, he maintained, ended in a positivism which was at once atheist, egoist, pessimist, and revolutionary. His act made a sensation. His hearers were captivated and immediately began to take sides for or against him.

In spite of his many adversaries he was nominated to a minor professorship at the University of Moscow. Thus at the age of twenty-one he began his career as a teacher. The opening words of his first lecture were characteristic: " In every sphere of his activity, and before all else, man dreams of liberty." It was a bold word in the Russia of those days, for it implied the curtailment of many a governmental activity. His development of the theme was, however, still bolder. The necessities of existence imposed on man three kinds of societies, an economic society

for the utilization of the material world, a political
society for the ordering of relations between man
and man, and a religious society for the due subordination of man to God.   Thus there is established
a *free theocracy*.   By this term Soloviev meant a
knowledge of the divine prerogatives, a consequent
love of them, and a free acceptance of them which
alone could bring real liberty.

Russia, however, was not yet ripe for such advanced thought. The young professor's success
was brilliant, but it led to jealousy and intrigues
against him.   After three months of teaching he
was removed from his chair.   He was not yet bad
enough for Siberia.   So he was silenced by being
sent upon a scientific mission to London and Paris.

The ostensible purpose of this journey was the
study of spiritism and cabalism.   In London, however, he occupied himself much with Anglicanism
and the question of reunion with the Orthodox
Church.   From London he went to France and Italy,
making his way to Egypt to study the beliefs of
the Arabs.   In the train he had his first experience
of Catholic clergy—two hundred and fifty of them
on their way to Rome.   " Fine fellows," he called
them, " and not one of them looked like a Jesuit."
On his return he spent a month in Italy and a fortnight in Paris.   It was in Paris that he first conceived the idea of a book on the *Principle of Universal
Religion*, an idea which fructified eventually in his
chief work, *Russia and the Universal Church*.   In
Paris, too, he met Renan, who made no better
mpression on him than that of " a vulgar boaster,"

By the beginning of 1877 the agitation against him had calmed down, so that he was allowed to return to Moscow. But almost immediately there was trouble. He was not minded to suppress the truth which was so dear to his heart, nor were his enemies minded to allow him to express it. A conference which he called *The Three Forces* was the occasion of his further persecution. His thesis was that mankind was influenced by three forces, a tendency towards social unity, a tendency towards individualism, and a higher tendency to respect God in other individuals and in their societies. The first tendency had been exaggerated by the Mussulman, with the result that he had become stagnated. The second had been exaggerated by the peoples of the West, with the result that their energies had become isolated almost to vanishing-point. The third tendency remained as something to be realized by the Slav of the East. Then would Russia live and be the leavening influence of the world.

Such a thesis, however, was pleasing to neither party. To the Slavophiles it was not exclusive enough. To the Occidentalists it was not revolutionary enough. Both parties, therefore, combined to have silence imposed on Soloviev and to have him sent into retirement.

By the intervention of friends an honourable retirement was found for him. He was appointed to a position on the Council of Education at Petrograd. The appointment was generally considered as a sort of reparation, but nevertheless it kept

Soloviev directly under the control of the authorities, and effectively hindered his liberty of speech.

Shortly afterwards he was nominated to a minor professorship in the Petrograd University, but his career there was even shorter than at Moscow. His thought was developing rapidly, and had now taken a direction leading straight towards Catholicism.

The embodiment of his thought took the shape of twelve *Lectures on Theandrism.* " Theandrism " was the companion word to his " Theocracy." By theocracy he meant a full and free acknowledgment of the rights and authority of God. Such an acknowledgment made us recognize God in His creatures, and led us to love our neighbours as ourselves. But all these traces of God in man were but sketches of the great divine appearance, when the Word was made flesh in the womb of a Virgin. Thus did the figurative theandrisms give way to the real theandrism, God made man in history. The purpose of this theandrism was that all men might become united to God. We are all called to be partakers of the divine nature. Thus there is now a universal theandrism, which is made up of the united multitude of participated theandrisms.

A savour of pantheism, perhaps, some will say. Soloviev, however, took pains to guard against this by declaring that the Man-God was one unique Person. Jesus Christ alone was the Word eternally begotten. And from Him, as from the Father, the Holy Ghost eternally proceeds. For a universal theandrism every man must be incorporated into

Christ. Every earthly activity must be subordinated to this end. The purpose of all societies,
civil and economic, is to serve the Kingdom of God,
the Church, the Universal Church, the Catholic
Church.

From the above it is evident that from his early
manhood Soloviev was fully convinced of the doctrine
of the *Filioque*. Living in the theological atmosphere
which he did, this alone must have been a tremendous
help to him in adjusting his ideas on the Universal
Church. As yet his concept of the Church was
wanting in definition, and indeed some of its lines
were very crooked in comparison with the objective
reality. Nevertheless he hoped to see a Universal
Church some day realized by an agreement between
the East and the West, and to bring about this
union became the ruling passion of his life.

One would have thought that the formulation of
his ideas would have been met with great favour by
the various authorities who were watching him.
For he maintained that the Eastern Church represented a Divine foundation, whilst the Western
represented only human weakness; and it was the
union of these two elements which would produce
a spiritualized humanity, a Universal Church.
But the proposal pleased no one. Conservatives
and Liberals conspired together for the removal
of Soloviev from the Petrograd University. And
within four months, namely in March, 1881, his
career as a professor was brought to a close, and
this time for ever.

In deference, however, to the Russian authorities,

we ought to say that it was not merely his abstract views on a Universal Church which caused him to be removed. These views fructified into certain practical conclusions of which the Russian State was bound to take notice. For instance, Soloviev protested against the frequent executions in Russia, and invited the new Tsar to give Christian example. He asked him, for instance, not to execute regicides, but to give them a chance of moral enlightenment and conversion. But Russia was not ready for such developments of the City of God.

Thenceforward to the end of his life Soloviev was refused all public utterance, except by way of writing which could be controlled by the censor. A few months before his death the University of Warsaw obtained permission to offer him a chair. The incident was useful as an indication of the growing tolerance of the Russian State, but it came too late to be of any service to Soloviev as a lecturer. Henceforward his life was that of a writer.

But even as a writer the censorship held him within what he believed too limited a sphere. He persevered as long as he could in his native tongue. But the annoyances became so frequent that he at length sought an outlet for his work in a foreign language. His first article outside Russia appeared in a Croatian journal, *Katolik List*, under the title *Eastern Church or Orthodox Church*. In all his evasions of the law, however, he remained loyal to the Tsar and to Russia. When he was charged with want of patriotism he replied that his patriotism was of a much better kind than was commonly supposed; for his love for Russia was not a blind love, blinding him to her faults, but a love which enabled him to love her in spite of her faults. Whilst loving her he condemned her acts of injustice. He longed for a greater and more beautiful Russia, less dominating and less violent. He wished for a Russia better ordered, more moral and more Christian—more truly worthy to be called Holy Russia. He hoped for a Russia influential less by its arms than by its faith and charity. He wanted a Russia that would develop the mystic body of Christ and that would glorify the only and holy Church of Jesus Christ.

In the past the hindrance to all religious progress had been the schism between the East and the West. Here, then, was his problem of the future. How could there be an Orthodoxy truly slavophile, yet obedient to the command to teach all nations ? To solve this question, Soloviev gave himself up to a systematic study of theology, at the same time keeping his philosophy in living contact with the question. Indeed it is remarkable how he made nearly every question he touched lead up to the theme of the Universal Church.

As a philosopher his thought divided naturally into two streams, the mental and the moral science. His treatise, *The Philosophical Principles of an Integral Science*, laid down the basis of his metaphysics. He maintained that nearly all contemporaneous philosophy treated the intellectual life with too much isolation. It had been rudely divorced from the life of man as a whole. Such a method, whether by way of Hegelianism, or of empiricism, would be sure to lead to scepticism. Moreover, such a method missed the supreme question of philosophy, namely: Whither does this life lead ?

Therefore Soloviev replied with his integralism or whole-man philosophy. In addition to the intelligence seeking the True, the full appropriation of reality involves a disposition of the will seeking the Good, and a quickened sensibility seeking the Beautiful. Thus was this integral philosophy in full communication with physical science on the one hand and speculative thought on the other. With such experience it could turn human reflection towards superhuman realities. It could mount up beyond human life, beyond cosmic life, until it reached the absolute Essence-Existence. As a moralist, Soloviev summed up his teaching in a work entitled, *The Justification of the Good.* His aim was to show his readers the real meaning of life. He proposed to them three questions: Has life got a reason for its existence ? Must one seek for the meaning of life in the moral order ? Does the higher flight into that which is spiritual require, permit, or exact a sacrifice of that which would be excess in physiological tendencies ?

We have said that Soloviev was one of the foremost examples of the modern mind. This is especially evident in his great work on morals. He not only showed the clearest grasp of the present situation, but also, like the English Newman, he showed a keen anticipation of the future.

First, he dealt with the pessimists who abandoned their lives to caprice, and who, when further satisfaction was not to be had, committed suicide. Even they bore witness to a higher meaning of life. They felt it and saw it, but they were too lazy to make the effort to reach it.

Then came the æsthetes of every kind. To them life had a meaning because it was a great force, because it had a grandeur and a beauty. Morality did not enter into such concepts. The moral life was inconvenient and uncomfortable. Beauty, however, was fascinating, and the grandeur of life exalted and quickened us. It was the doctrine of the strong man set up by Nietzsche: " Slaves can adore a God Who makes Himself man and humbles Himself. But the strong adore only their own ascent to the superman, the endless progression of human beauty, human grandeur, and human power."

But, replied Soloviev, that endless progression ends in a corpse. Instead of beauty you have putrefaction. The inexorable fact of death reduces the body's beauty and grandeur and power to nothing. Christianity, on the contrary, is not founded upon death, but upon the First-born from the dead, and real beauty, grandeur, and power could only be found in the Absolute Good.

Such is the general trend of the work, the final aim being " the perfect organization of an integral humanity." And such organization postulated a Universal Church. Thus the philosopher has all unconsciously transformed himself into a theologian.

Yet not unconsciously, for he is careful to notice
that the superhuman is not acquired by natural
science, having need of a special communication.
" This communication, willed by God, opens to our
thought a new sphere of studies and contemplations:
the intimate deeps of divinity become accessible
to theology and the mystical life." Henceforward,
therefore, theology was to claim a larger share of
his attention. And he needed it. He was so
extremely nationalist, so thoroughly imbued with
slavophile ideas, that he thought the Christian
restoration of the world was reserved for Russia
and the Orthodox Church. The Western Church
had dwelt too much on the material element of
the Incarnation, propagating the faith by force,
and thinking more of ecclesiastical domination than
the love of Christ. And as for the Reformation,
although it fought against these abuses, yet it was
itself poisoned with Western individualism, and
shrunk into sheer rationalism. Soloviev, in a
word, had just that view of " Romanism " which
was traditional and current in the East.

Nevertheless he resolved to face an independent
inquiry into the value of the Roman Catholic claims.
He gave himself up to the volumes of Mansi and
Migne. The Councils and the Fathers were the
sources whence he sought the truth. He made a
Russian translation of the *Didache*, claiming, in
his introduction, that it showed how Providence
was always allied to a perpetual hierarchy and the
dogma of the sacraments. The due developments
of these doctrines, therefore, were not novelties

invented by the Catholic Church, as the Orthodox Church asserted.

Once again the enemies of Soloviev were roused. He went forward, however, and even ventured to censure the spiritual power in Russia. He blamed the Holy Synod for the sin of inaction. At the same time he delivered a counter-blast against the Roman Catholic Church. In the West, he said, the Papacy had set up the Pope in place of Christ, and Protestantism had hunted out Christ. Orthodox Russia alone, up to the eighteenth century, had respected the liberty of souls. The separation of the East from the West ought never to have taken place. The evil wrought by Constantinople should be repaired by Russia. Having grown up and become conscious of herself, Russia should no longer continue the historic sin of Constantinople. Rome was thoroughly Christian because she was universal. Let us not exaggerate her faults.

Then he issued his important work: *The Great Conflict and Christian Politics.* The conflict, of course, was that between the East and the West. It was not essentially a religious conflict, but one of radical tendencies. The East was contemplative, and in this guise yielded itself to every form of inactivity. The West was active, and in this guise yielded itself to the merely human. The Incarnation restrained the two tendencies. Nevertheless they were the real cause of the schism of 1054: the *Filioque* was but the pretext. Pride and ambition, he maintained, had caused the Popes to restore the old Cæsarism. That was not the authority with

2

which the Church of Christ should be ruled. " The word *Caput Ecclesiæ*," he wrote, " cannot be applied to all the Popes; only those have merited it in whom Christian humanity has been able to recognize the Eternal Pontiff." The book caused a big sensation. Its purpose was immediately turned into a political direction. Soloviev was charged with agitating on behalf of Poland !

A refutation of the work was attempted by the Archpriest A. M. Ivantzov-Platanov. Soloviev replied with nine leading questions. These were intended rather for the whole Russian hierarchy. But they reached much farther. They travelled as far as Rome, and were made the subject of a conference by Cardinal Mazzella.

There was now an active communication set up between Soloviev and certain representative Catholics. Soloviev wrote to Bishop Strossmayer of Bosnia and Sirmium, asking for an interview either at Agram or Djakovo. The Russian police, however, were on the watch. They interrupted his plans, and for six months prevented him from leaving the country. But on June 29, 1886, he managed to arrive at Vienna, and from there wrote immediately to Bishop Strossmayer. The Bishop welcomed him as his guest at Djakovo, where he remained for two months. Both host and guest were enthusiastically slavophile, a circumstance which enabled them to come near together in their discussions on the cause of reunion.

Yet with all his good intentions towards Rome Soloviev asserted his constancy towards Russia

and the Church of Russia. Writing to Bishop
Strossmayer on his way home, he enclosed a memorandum in which he declared that after the reunion
" the superior position which always belonged to
the Eastern Church, and which now in Russia
belonged to the Orthodox Emperor, should remain
intact."

This memorandum marked a new direction for
Soloviev. He understood that henceforward his
mission in life was, at the cost of every personal
sacrifice, to work for an agreement between Russia
and the Catholic Church. He would show by his
example that a Slav could and ought, whilst remaining a Slav, to widen his heart and soul towards
Catholic faith and zeal, and prove that Roman
Catholicism completed, crowned and unified all
that was legitimate in the traditional Orthodoxy
of the East.

For the realization of this idea he planned a large
work in three volumes, to which he gave the title of
The History and Future of Theocracy. But only
one volume saw the light. The censor refused
permission to print. Soloviev again had recourse
to a foreign publisher. After having made certain
excisions in the hope that the book might be admitted
to Russia, he issued it at Agram. But the compromise was ineffective; the book was prohibited.
Soloviev now felt that it was waste of time to write
any further in Russian for the Russians. He must
try a more roundabout way. So he began a new
work in French, one which proved to be his greatest
and most effectual: *Russia and the Universal Church.*

The fundamental thesis of this, which embodied his one aim in life, might be stated as follows: " The Universal Church is founded on the truth affirmed by our faith. Since truth is one, the true faith must also be one. And since the unity of faith does not reside really and directly in the whole body of the faithful, it must be sought in the lawful authority residing in one head—authority having the guarantee of divine assistance—and thus received with love and confidence by all the faithful."* And the first step in the explication of the thesis was " to establish a moral and intellectual bond between the religious conscience of Russia and the truth of the Universal Church." His hope lay in the simple Russian people. He drew a big distinction between the intellectuals and officials on the one hand and the multitude on the other. The latter, he maintained, were really Catholic in their faith and piety. It was the official theologians who were so anti-Catholic.

A work of less importance, though perhaps of more topical interest at the present moment, is the one which has lately been offered to the English-speaking public. Its correct title is: *War, Progress, and the End of History : Three Discussions.* Two English translations have appeared during the past year, one issued by the University of London Press under the aforesaid title, the other issued by Constable under the title: *War and Christianity from the Russian point of view : Three Conversations.*

The book was written as an antidote to Tolstoï.

---

* *La Russie et l'Eglise universetle*, Paris, 1889, p. 93.

The question of militarism was exercising people's minds. Tolstoï had been writing against war, and with such effect that men were resenting conscription. Officers even were known to have been ashamed of the army and to have given up their profession in consequence. Tolstoï had, in fact, created an impression that war had no moral defence.

Soloviev came forward as the champion of his country's cause. He was quite as good a Slav as Tolstoï—and a much better disputant. Tolstoï had preached from the text: "Resist not him that is evil, but whosoever smiteth thee on the right cheek, turn to him the other also." From that he had inferred that the use of physical force in the settlement of disputes showed a desire to do evil, and therefore was wrong.

The logical outcome of such teaching required the abrogation of all military and police arrangements. Soloviev saw in this nothing but the downfall of European civilization, and its replacement by a Pan-Mongolism. So he asks: "Can reason and conscience count up to three?" If so, then they must see how wrong it is for number one to stand by, whilst number two persecutes the innocent number three.

This argument he embodies in an imaginary conversation, which takes place between five Russians in a garden on the shores of the Mediterranean. An old General, a politician, a young prince, a lady of middle age, and Mr. Z. make up the company. The prince is obviously meant for

Tolstoï, and Mr. Z. for Soloviev himself. The General, who is the chief speaker in the first conversation, tells the story of one of his exploits in the Russo-Turkish War. A large party of Bashi-Bazouks had sacked an Armenian village, committing unspeakable atrocities. " I could not mention," says the General, " all the details. One picture is clear in my eyes at this moment—a woman lying on her back on the ground, her neck and shoulders tied to the cart-wheel in such a way that she could not turn her head, and she lay there neither burnt nor broken, but with a ghastly twisted expression on her face—she had evidently died from terror. In front of her was a high pole stuck into the ground, and a naked baby was tied to it—probably her own son—all black with fire and its eyes protruding."

With Cossacks and artillery he set out in pursuit and overtook them. First one Cossack and then another rolled over, until at length the eldest centurion came to him and asked: " Order us to attack, Excellency ! Otherwise anathema will fall upon us before we get the artillery into position." " Be patient, darlings," he replies, " just for a little. I know you can scatter them, but what sweetness is there in that ? God orders me to make an end of them, not to scatter them."

And he did make an end of them. " God blessed all my six cannon. It was the one occasion in my life when I experienced a complete moral satisfaction. My act remains till now, and will of course remain for ever, my purest memory. Well, and that one good act of mine was a murder, and not by any means a small murder, for in a quarter of an hour I killed considerably more than a thousand men. . . . Certainly I did not kill with my hands, with these sinful hands, but with the aid of six pure, sinless, steel cannon, with the most virtuous and beneficial shrapnel."

Of course, he is speaking ironically when he calls it murder, using the terminology of the pacificists. But in this way he deals blow after blow against the Tolstoï position.

The curious thing is that the question of the military power of Russia brought Soloviev once again to the question of Rome. The concluding pages of the *Three Discussions* are an allegory of the end of history. Through the centuries the union of Rome and Russia has not been accomplished, but now at the end of time it is clamouring for consummation.

Soloviev used the political situation of the time to symbolize the spiritual. Japan was made to represent the kingdom of Antichrist, whilst Russia represented the Kingdom of Christ. With remarkable foresight Soloviev prophesied the defeat of Russia by Japan, the realization of which event gave point to his visions of the future Church, and made him a prophet accepted in his own country. There was an Antichrist and an Antipope, and Tolstoï himself was pictured as one of the forerunners of Antichrist. These drew the multitudes after them and victory seemed to be on their side.

Only a few Christians remained faithful to the true Christ, the Catholics led by Pope Peter II., the

Orthodox by the venerable John, and the Protestants by one Professor Ernest Pauli. The company, all told, numbered twelve. They assembled together " in the darkness of the night on a high and lonely place," on the barren hills near Jericho, and then and there was the union of the Churches accomplished.

Soloviev, therefore, was keenly conscious of the many obstacles which were in the way of the object for which he laboured, and of the time it must take before it could be realized. He seemed to know that his own end was not far distant, for he leaves his allegory unfinished—the writer, he said, wished to write more when he got better. But he did not get well, and the end of the tale was buried with him in the Danilof monastery. Soloviev, as a matter of fact, died suddenly a few weeks later at the age of forty-seven on a journey to see his mother.

But what about his own conversion? Long, long ago he had sung his " Lead, Kindly Light ":

" Beneath the morning mists I went with trembling footsteps towards the enchanted land—shores full of mystery. The crimson of the dawn put out the stars; my dreams still hovered round me, and my soul, still wrapped in them, prayed to the Unknown God.

" In the white freshness of the day I walk, always alone, through an undiscovered country. The mists disperse. Mine eyes see clear ahead—how steep the mountain path is, and how far away everything still seems—everything that I have dreamed!

"Until nightfall will I go; marching with un-wearied stride to the long-desired shore, where, under the light of the early stars and in the blaze of triumphal fires, glows on the mountain top the temple that was promised me—the home that shall be mine."

But did the mist clear away, and did the temple of the Church reveal itself to his vision? During the later years of his life and for some years after his death certain doubts have prevailed concerning this. Nor have reasons for the doubts been wanting. First there was some necessity for keeping the matter secret. Soloviev had been warned that if he left Paris to enter Russia he would surely be arrested and deported. Orders had actually been given for his internment in a monastery in Archangel. Hence there was need of a prudent silence. Then after his death his relations who remained Orthodox were at pains to show that he had never become Catholic.

At length, however, the full truth came out. On February 18, 1896, he was received into the Catholic Church by a convert priest, M. Nicolas Tolstoï. The event took place in the chapel of Notre Dame de Lourdes at Moscow in the presence of the members of M. Tolstoï's family and of several eminent people of Petrograd and Moscow. The priest was arrested next day, but managed to evade prosecution, and a few days later was in Rome to report the conversion to Pope Leo XIII.

Soloviev had ever stood for the privileges of the Eastern rites, and now he made it quite clear that in joining the Catholic Church he was not joining

the Latin rite. He, therefore, made a profession
of faith which he had fixed upon long before the
time came to make it:

" As a member of the real and venerable Orthodox
Eastern or Greek-Russian Church which speaks
neither by an anti-canonical synod nor by the
servants of the secular power . . . I acknowledge
as supreme judge in matters of religion . . . the
Apostle Peter who lives in his successors, and has
not heard in vain the words of the Saviour: Thou
art Peter and upon this rock I will build My Church
—confirm thy brethren—feed My sheep, feed My
lambs."

On his deathbed, however, he could not obtain
the services of either a priest of the Uniate rite or
of the Latin rite. So he availed himself of the
services of the village curé who happened to be
of the Orthodox rite. This he was quite entitled
to do, for every validly ordained priest has jurisdiction at the hour of death. One thing, however,
is quite certain, namely, that when Soloviev for
the last time confessed his sins, he retracted none
of his theological judgments. He died in full
communion with Rome.

After his death the Russian authorities removed
the ban from his works, and now the voice of the
apostle of the Universal Church, although silent,
begins to speak, and the sound thereof becomes
ever more and more audible. Just as in the West
we have Newman societies, so in the East there are
Soloviev societies, formed for the study and pro-
pagation of his ideals. And if in the past the

Russian Government has shown so much opposition to a pioneer of Catholicism, and now tolerates him and gives him freedom, let us take hope for the future. Big institutions always move slowly, and Russia is a very big institution.

CHAPTER I

NEWMAN AND SOLOVIEV

At first sight there seems to be little resemblance between the great English Cardinal and the so-called Russian Newman. Further consideration, however, will show that their chief points of difference may be reduced to two—Soloviev was never a priest, either before or after his conversion to Catholicism, and his compatriots never knew with certainty whether it was on account of the liturgical ceremonies that he sought admission to the Church of Rome. He personally was convinced that he had at no period been completely outside her fold, but thought that the Slavonic nations were not absolutely cut off from the Church, because the historic excommunication affected Constantinople and not Russia. For instance, in 1888 he wrote: " Russia is not formally and regularly separated from the Catholic Church. It occupies in this respect an abnormal and undecided position, eminently favourable to reunion. The false and anti-Catholic doctrines, taught in our seminaries and theological colleges are not binding upon the Russian Church as a whole, nor do they in any way affect the faith of the people. The government of

29

the Russian Church is illegal, schismatical, condemned (*lata sententia*) by the third canon of the seventh Œcumenical Council; it is rejected by a considerable number of orthodox Russians (the Old Believers), and is tolerated in a half-hearted fashion by the rest. It is unfair to blame the Russian nation for the Cæsaropapism under which it groans, and against which it never ceases to protest. Men like Pobedonostsev and Tolstoï are no more representative of Russia than men such as Floquet, Goblet, and Freycinet are of France."

Soloviev used to refer, in support of his theory, to the attitude adopted by Mgr. (afterwards Cardinal) Vannutelli, at the time of his legation to Moscow in 1883. For a member of the Russian Church to embrace Catholicism two things only were, in his opinion, necessary—viz., to reject the anti-canonical claims of the Sacred Synod, and to submit to the jurisdiction and infallible authority of the Pope. Under existing circumstances, since the Slav Uniate rite, being forbidden by the Russian Government, could not be established in the empire, Soloviev thought that it would be a mistake to require anything further, because it would involve disobedience to the pontifical laws against the latinization of Orientals, and would justify the calumnious statement that Rome cherishes an undying hostility to the holy and venerable traditions of the East. To the end of his life he desired that the members of the Orthodox Church in Russia should be permitted to submit directly to the Holy See, without being forced, or even allowed, to go through any canonical formality.

Soloviev's profession of faith was as complete as Newman's, and bore no resemblance to Pusey's timid hesitation. The anguish of mind that preceded it, and the ostracism that followed it, were not unlike Newman's trials. Both felt at first a strong prejudice against the Papacy, and in the case of each this prejudice was overcome by loyalty to religion, fervour in prayer, desire to see the light, and resolution to do God's will. Both suffered keenly when they felt it to be their duty to give up the instruction of others; Newman ceased his sermons in St Mary's at Oxford, and Soloviev was removed from his lectureship in Petrograd.

It is no easy task to analyze the more subtle points of likeness between these two men. Each possessed the soul of a philosopher; each was an intuitive theologian, an artist, and a scholar; each had deep affections and perfect purity. Their tastes seem to have been identical; they both loved Holy Scripture and the Fathers, especially St. Augustine; both studied ecclesiastical history and the philosophy of religious development, both strove to raise human knowledge to God, and to inculcate the daily duties of religion. Both, even before their conversion, pledged themselves to perpetual celibacy; both were impelled to sacrifice earthly friendships that they might follow Christ; both were so passionately enamoured of their country and the Catholic Church as to offer themselves to undergo any suffering, if only a reconcili-

ation could be effected between these objects of
their love.

A man's mind often affects his outward appearance and expression, and those who knew Newman
in his younger days might have discovered some
likeness to him in the description of Soloviev at
the age of twenty-three, given by the Vicomte de
Vogüé, after meeting him for the first time in 1876,
at the house of M. de Lesseps in Cairo.   De Vogüé
writes: " Soloviev has one of those faces that can
never be forgotten; he has fine regular features,
his face is thin and pale, surrounded by long, curly
hair.   His eyes are wonderful, piercing and thought-
ful.   He seems to be an idea clothed in flesh, of
the type of the Slav Christ depicted by the monks
on old ikons, one who loves in spite of calumny and
suffering.   Soloviev is a dialectician and a dreamer;
frank as a child, complex as a woman, perplexing,
attractive, and indescribable."

Fifty years earlier a familiar figure in the streets
of Oxford was that of a young clergyman, wearing
a shabby long coat; he was thin and pale, and stooped
a little, his eyes were large and flashing, but he gave
the impression of being frail and delicate.   He
generally walked quickly, absorbed in thought, or
else engaged in conversation with some friend.
This Englishman certainly bore some resemblance
to the Russian whom Eugène Tavernier met in
Paris in 1888, at the house of the Princess von
Sayn-Wittgenstein, and whom he describes as
" very tall and thin, with splendid eyes, marvellously
gentle, clear, and piercing, in spite of being short-

sighted. His manner was unassuming and somewhat shy; his speech revealed his energetic daring and firmness; his voice was expressive, deep, and full of startling inflections, now serious, now caressing. A mind characteristically French was as natural to him as to a Parisian."

Soloviev's life was much shorter than Newman's —he died at an age when Newman was still at Littlemore, but his influence in Russia is nevertheless very great. During his lifetime "many called him a prophet, sometimes in jest, sometimes in earnest; but now we can see that the service which he rendered us was in very truth that of a prophet, and, although he was at first misunderstood and ridiculed in his own country, he is becoming more highly appreciated year by year." The above words, written by S. N. Boulgakov in 1903, are more true now than then. Soloviev's works have had a powerful influence upon the trend of philosophical and religious thought in Russia, and this influence continues to increase Before, however, he was in a position to exert it, he was himself moulded and impressed by his surroundings, and in order to gain a correct opinion of him, we must look at his environment, and consider in broad outlines the prevailing tendencies of Russian thought between 1850 and 1880. When we have done this, we shall perceive the circumstances that formed his character, and shall be able to appreciate his originality. The study of his personality will disclose the historical importance of his work, and will perhaps throw some light upon

3

the probable course of the movement that he initiated.

We can draw upon Soloviev himself for a description of the state of Russia during this period. He often dealt with this subject, and treated it fully in his *National Question in Russia*, as well as in numerous articles, such as *The Russian National Ideal* and *The Historical Sphinx, Byzantinism and Russia*. From the moment of their publication, his opinions aroused much discussion, but he never abandoned them.

Prejudice and excessive attention to detail have caused many to overlook the truth of an independent synthesis, which may even now astonish some Russians. They would do well, however, to note that the following pages do not contain any preconceived system devised by a foreigner, but the opinions expressed by a Russian thinker, whose patriotism is beyond question, and whose views have often been proved correct by subsequent events. The very severity of his judgments will emphasize the progress already made by Russia during the past few years.

CHAPTER II

THE INFLUENCE OF TOLSTOÏ AND TCHADAÏEV

SOLOVIEV'S first essay was written in 1873, a year
that marks the centre of a period during which
Russia achieved great success in her foreign policy,
but began to lose her vital energy through internal
disputes. The German Emperor was solemnly received at Petrograd, and his nephew, Alexander II.,
congratulated him publicly on having established
a new empire, and exacted vengeance for the misfortunes of the Crimean War. Since the latest
rebellion in Poland had been crushed, just before
the insurrections destined to deliver the Christian
Slavs of the south from the Turkish yoke, Russia
seemed to dominate the East, just as Germany was
supreme in the West of Europe—she had regained
her diplomatic and military prestige in the eyes of
foreign nations.

On the other hand, signs of disturbance were increasing in the interior. Tolstoï's influence had
revealed to the masses and to individuals their
secret grievances. The evil was not the direct
result of his teaching, but each reader suspected
its existence in himself and others. During an
epidemic, the mere description of contagious dis-

35

eases tends, doubtless, to spread them, and a book
on medicine may, at such a time, be dangerous to
people with a morbid imagination. In the same
way Tolstoï's works aggravated the sense of individual suffering, or actually caused it by way of
suggestion. Everyone thought that, because all
men suffered, he himself was suffering; everyone
felt pity for his own lot; did not Count Tolstoï
grieve over the misery of Russia ?

We must not, however, exaggerate. M. Radlov,
Soloviev's venerable friend, wrote the following
remark in his *Biographical Notes on Soloviev :*
" Tolstoï certainly contributed towards checking
the influence of materialism in Russia, and developing interest in religious questions." We may readily
endorse this opinion, and we shall see how Soloviev
himself was at first affected by German materialism,
that for a long time predominated in Russia, whilst
laity and clergy alike displayed total indifference
to religious thought. On minds and hearts thus
poisoned with indifferentism, Tolstoï's works acted
in many cases as an antidote. Nevertheless, an
anti-Christian movement is associated with the
name of Tolstoï, although his fame is greater in
the West than among his own countrymen, to
whom many of his creations appear unreal and
fanciful.

We are perhaps too apt to believe that he personi-
fies every type of Russian character, that his heroes
and their actions represent accurately the psychology
of individuals and social realities, and that the
paradoxes of his gospel, built on clouds with fantastic

outlines, would form collectively the ideal of every Slav thinker, whether simple or refined.

Men of intellect in Petrograd and Moscow do not share all our enthusiasm; they acknowledge Tolstoï's merits as a writer and his generous sacrifices as a man; they admire the painful accuracy of his descriptions, the precision of his analysis, and the purity of his style, but at the present time they criticize him as a thinker, condemn his theories, and resist his influence.

This resistance hardly existed in 1873, and we cannot estimate all the depressing results of Tolstoï's teaching, which was the more disastrous because it found justification in facts. We are told that he is not the incarnation of Russia, and it is true; he and the characters in his books are Russian, but they do not stand alone. Karataïev, Gricha, and Vronsky are drawn from nature, but there are many other types besides these; and it may be that Tolstoï's influence will be fleeting, like that of Nihilism, and we should judge Russia unfairly if we looked at it altogether from his point of view; we might as well examine it through a telescope, the object-glass of which was directed towards the smoke of bombs. Russia deserves better treatment than this.

The foregoing remarks would certainly not have been accurate during the stormy period between 1860 and 1885. Then, indeed, both individuals and society in general seemed only too often incapable of distinguishing good from evil; in fact, they were not far from regarding right and wrong as identical. As early as 1830 Count Peter Tchadaïev (1794-1856), a very original thinker and a true forerunner of Soloviev, had a presentiment of this misfortune. In a letter written at Moscow on December 1, 1829, he says: " We are all deficient in enterprise, method, and logic, and the syllogism of the West is unknown to us. Yet there is something more than frivolity in our best intellects, although our noblest ideas, for want of connection and sequence, are productive of nothing, and remain paralyzed in our brains." And again: " Ours is the recklessness of a life without experience or foresight, which is connected with nothing but the ephemeral existence of an individual isolated from his species. . . . We have absolutely no idea of what is general; everything is to us particular, vague, and incomplete."

Such statements, like all satires, are exaggerated, but contain an element of truth. Until towards the end of the nineteenth century, philosophical thought seemed incapable of growth in Russia. In these circumstances philosophy is unknown, and this lack of general culture allows all sorts of follies to run riot; minds have to choose between being poisoned or dying of starvation.

The philosophism of the eighteenth century supplied no remedy for the evil, since it contained very little real philosophy, and this little remained something foreign to the Russian mind, not being its product, and not penetrating to its depths.

There were the same defects in the pseudo-scholasticism of the Orthodox seminaries. Derived

as it was from miserable German school-books of
1730, it was still further impoverished by the
elimination of everything distinctively Catholic or
Protestant in tone.   No Russian element was added
to supplement this defective teaching, and no
effort at adaptation enabled the Russian mind to
assimilate it.   There was nothing but a Latin
handbook, dry and unintelligible; and scholasticism
has thus always been caricatured in Russia, so
that it is easy to understand why it fell into disfavour, and is still regarded with contempt by men
of the highest intelligence.   Philosophy became a
synonym for incoherence, and under such conditions
it was bound to perish, and its final disappearance
was effected by the reform of 1840, which required
it to be taught in Russian and not in Latin.   The
name, indeed, continued to appear in the syllabus,
and no one noticed that it stood for nothing.   We
can hardly say that philosophy disappeared, for
it had never been anything but a name in Russia.

Very few perceived the danger of an education
that filled the brain with knowledge without culti-
vating the intellect.   Words learnt by heart, lists .
of events, etc., cannot replace human thought,
and the least spark may cause an explosion where
gunpowder is loosely stored.

Tchadaïev wrote: "Where are our scholars,
our thinkers ?   Who amongst us has ever thought
at all and who is thinking for us to-day ?"   He
was in a pessimistic mood when he said: "There
is something in our blood averse to all true progress.
We live only that our remote descendants, who

understand what it is, may learn a great lesson from us." But perhaps he did not exaggerate when he remarked to his contemporaries: " Isolated as we are in the world, we have given it nothing, we have taught it nothing; we have not added a single idea to the body of human thought; we have contributed nothing to the progress of the human mind, and we have disfigured all that this progress has bestowed on us. Since the first moment of our social existence, nothing has emanated from us for the common good of mankind; not one useful thought has been produced by the barren soil of our country; not one great truth has flashed out from our midst; we never have taken the trouble to imagine anything ourselves, and from what others have imagined we have borrowed only deceptive appearances and useless luxury."

This passage, unfortunately, was brought to the notice of Nicholas I., with terrible results. The Tsar wrote on the margin of the manuscript three words only: " Is he mad ?" but the courtiers went further, and Tchadaïev was forthwith deprived of all his degrees and appointments. The Court physician was ordered to visit him daily to report on his mental condition, until the count was reduced to writing the *Apology of a Madman*, dedicated to the Emperor.

Under the burden of his misfortunes Schelling's pupil turned his attention to the study of Christianity, and there can be no doubt that what he wrote then regarding the universal influence of Christ and His work contributed towards the conversion to Catholicism of his old pupil, Prince Gagarin. The latter, who subsequently became a Jesuit, did much to restore his master's reputation by publishing a selection from the works of this first Russian thinker. At the present time Tchadaïev, once regarded as a maniac, is studied, admired, and respected, almost as if he were a prophet.

Soloviev had much in common with Tchadaïev, though he went further, and rendered the ideas, derived from his predecessor, more precise and complete. Soloviev concerned himself with synthesis and deductions; Tchadaïev was contented to express his occasionally very remarkable intuitions regarding the philosophy of history. Let us consider two or three instances in which he served as a model to Soloviev.

On the subject of the dignity of thought before and after the time of Christ he wrote: " There is nothing more simple than the glory of Socrates, the only man in the ancient world to die for his convictions. This unique example of heroism could not but amaze the men of his nation (materialistic Greeks). But is it not foolish for us to misunderstand him as they did, when we have seen whole nations lay down their life for the sake of truth ?"

In 1898 Soloviev wrote: " By his death Socrates displayed all the moral force of which pure humanity is capable; anything further requires the supernatural strength of Him who has power to rise again to everlasting life. The weakness and downfall of the ' divine ' Plato show that man cannot make himself superhuman by means of thought, genius, and moral purpose; none but a God-man can do this."

Tchadaïev was fond of tracing Christ's influence upon non-Christians, and says: " No one can have a clear idea of the great work of redemption, nor comprehend the mysteries of Christ's reign on earth, unless he sees the action of Christianity wherever the Saviour's name is uttered, and realizes that His influence affects every mind which, in one way or another, is brought into contact with His doctrines."

This line of thought led to a universalist or Catholic conclusion, which inevitably had something to do with Prince Gagarin's conversion, and which was to Soloviev a source of inspiration. Elsewhere Tchadaïev writes: " Nothing more plainly reveals the divine origin of this religion than this characteristic of absolute universality, which enables it to affect men in every possible way, taking possession unawares of their minds, dominating and controlling them, even when they seem to resist most stoutly, by introducing to them truths previously unknown, by inspiring emotions hitherto unfelt, and imparting thoughts that bring them, though they know it not, into the general order."

Russians of the present day call Soloviev the first national philosopher, but philosophical reflection had at least been attempted by his predecessor, Count Tchadaïev, who, however, long remained unappreciated, and died in 1856, when the man who was to win him recognition was only three years old. In 1862 the Archimandrite professor Féodor was expelled from the ranks of the clergy for having expressed opinions tinged with Tchadaïev's philosophy.

After Tchadaïev there were a few poets, novelists, and some sincerely religious men like Khomiakov, the élite of Orthodox Russia in the middle of the nineteenth century, who studied the aspirations of the Slavs. At first sight the Slavs are a quiet race, very uniform in character, but in reality they are restless and varied. Their feelings are in a kind of irregular ebb and flow, and sudden storms follow long periods of calm. Outbursts of rage in individuals and rebellions among the masses are rare, but terrible when they occur. There is still an underlying current of barbarism and fanaticism in the race. Many students have been contented with a superficial examination of the Russian character; they are struck by the spirit of apathy and resignation, and do not fathom the depth of hidden feeling. Yet it is in the restless subconsciousness that storms arise; and there, for the last sixty years, a steady movement has been going on, very slow at first, but becoming more perceptible year by year; the hoary mass of ancestral traditions is slowly but surely yielding to the pressure of the Western nations, and more than once it has seemed on the point of giving way altogether, as though the house had been built on sand, and not on a rock.

A spectacle such as this impels men to reflect. At the end of the nineteenth century several Russians attempted to philosophize, some with considerable success, but their influence was invariably limited

to a narrow circle, and of them all Soloviev alone is
widely known. In spite of the attacks of jealous
rivals, his fame now surpasses that of all the rest,
and he tends to eclipse them altogether.

For a long time there was in Russia much opposition to Soloviev's prestige and activity in the
direction of reform. Towards the middle of the
nineteenth century utilitarians and Utopians formed
two antagonistic camps, and, in spite of all remonstrances on the part of some few serious thinkers,
they adopted two opposite lines of action, both
equally extreme and intolerant. The one party
aimed at copying the Western nations, and was
known as that of the Occidentalists, whereas the
Slavophile party clung to its own national traditions.
The latter refused to have anything to do with the
West, or to abandon any ancestral custom, and so
it enjoyed proud isolation both in politics and
religion, and insisted upon absolute immobility in
education and legislation. It called itself the
Nationalist party, and although it could not require
all its adherents to be believers, it forced them, by
its veneration for the past, to struggle in defence of
national and anti-Roman Orthodoxy. A decided
but judicious scheme of social and religious reform
had been already drawn up by a few clear-sighted
politicians, some reformers who understood the true
interests of their country and some sincere Christians.
All these desired to give fresh life to national
thought and activity by bringing them into touch
with the best elements of Western life, if it could

be done gradually and without causing any violent upheaval. These reformers quickly drew upon themselves the hostility of the extreme Nationalists. At the beginning of their conflict, members of both parties continued to meet in society, but in course of time the most noisy and violent spirits prevailed over men who held more moderate opinions. Being confronted with the most bigoted Slavophiles, the other party inevitably went further in the opposite direction, and in its turn displayed more enthusiasm than wisdom. This was deeply regretted by the prudent members of the party, but after 1860 their influence waned entirely.

The programme put forward by the Occidentalists was, in its way, as simple as that of the most rabid Slavophiles. Under the pretext of evolution and progress, it aimed at a universal overthrow of the existing state of affairs. It made positivism its excuse for violent efforts to destroy authority and level all inequalities; there was to be no *tchin*, no Tsar, no empire, and the liberty of the individual was to take the place of organized society. The leaders of the Occidentalist movement had lately proclaimed their wish to have no purely national Church, fatally enslaved to the civil power. Those who claimed to be their followers declared that they would not have any Church at all. The "Young Liberals," both doctrinaires and revolutionaries, condemned alike every form of Christianity, resisted every sign of a Christian spirit, and went so far as to assert dogmatically, in the name of their party, the incompatibility of science and faith.

They held that the modern spirit produced by positivism would destroy all religion, but especially all the religions known as positive. Most of the Slavophile party were connected with the Government, and thus they were supported by the force of the State and the influence of the State Church; they traded upon the traditional passivity of the masses.

The Liberals occupied almost all the chairs at the Universities, and so possessed a means of propaganda valuable everywhere, but of almost incalculable importance in a country where all other free manifestation of thought is proscribed. They were the scientific party, and had every opportunity of appealing to the critical tastes of an aristocracy which had come into contact with Western nations, of stirring up excitement among noisy or frivolous students, and of taking the lead among a half-educated middle-class, that followed them like a flock of sheep. Open hostilities soon broke out, and the two parties engaged in skirmishes almost every day. Their chiefs conceived a deadly hatred of one another—the expression is not exaggerated—and only the more moderate were satisfied with sending their rivals to Siberia, whilst the rank and file in each camp assumed an attitude of bitter antagonism.

Men of the same nation, who hardly knew one another, were always ready to welcome and to spread any calumny likely to bring their opponents into disrepute or ridicule. They were divided on every point save one—hostility to Rome. Rome insisted upon the universality of the Church, whereas the Russian national spirit was determined to enforce everywhere, even in the service of God, the isolation of one chosen race. This principle was described as racial independence. Rome stood at the head of the most vigorous and prolific organization of Christians, and the boldest leaders of Russian liberalism were bent upon destroying Christianity root and branch.

" Resistance to the encroachments of Rome " was the only war-cry raised by all Russians, regardless of party, though the truces between them became less frequent, and of shorter duration, as time went on.

Otherwise the line of division was unbroken, and there was no *via media* between the two extreme parties; unbelievers and Orthodox alike adopted as their motto the words " He that is not with me is against me "—words intelligible enough when uttered by One whose wisdom is infallible, but almost blasphemous when used to support the institutions of a man like Peter the Great or indigenous superstitions. Yet neither Liberals nor Slavophiles troubled about such considerations, and did not hesitate on every occasion to employ this imperious and autocratic formula.

Vladimir Soloviev felt the incongruity more than once, and often complained bitterly that in each camp theory and practice were in constant conflict; but his complaints for a long time attracted no attention. Even when this contradiction was pointed out, no one troubled about it. Was party

spirit to be put aside for such a trifle ? What did
contradictions matter ? Each was fighting for his
own ideas, and that was enough. Could they be
required to search deeply into these ideas and bring
them into harmony, and then take them as a rule
for conduct ? Such were the replies given to
Soloviev.

The tactics and systems of both parties were
indeed incoherent and contradictory, but no one
seemed disturbed or surprised at it. In spite of
their claims to stability, the Slavophiles strayed
into unforeseen paths and pursued in all directions
incongruous traces of a past that had never had
any real existence. Their vivid imaginations caused
the imperfections of the true past to disappear, and,
with complete disregard of chronology, they viewed
it in a manner both historically inaccurate and
logically incoherent. They had to select certain
features of the past for revival, and the selection
was carried on secretly; the features that did not
find favour were rejected unconditionally. For
instance, the most ardent admirers of all the national
traditions of Christianity tried to crush with their
anathemas and judicial decisions certain Christian
sects, essentially Slav, that were known as Staro-
veres, and consisted of Old Ritualists or Old
Believers.

On the other hand, striding across the centuries,
they put in juxtaposition all the remains that took
their fancy; they dug up relics of bygone ages,
and imagined that, by dint of decking an old trunk
with flowers stored up in some herbarium since the

tenth century, they could impart to the tree a life
that should be unchanging and eternal.

There were similar contradictions among the
extreme Neo-Occidentalists, who would fain have
cut down the tree in order, forsooth, to give more
freedom to its parts, and more life to its cells and
tissues. They spoke only of evolution, but the
changes that they desired would have involved dis-
integration. They wished to make progress, but
the absolute equality, that they aimed at imposing
upon all, would have killed all spontaneity and
hindered all development and movement.

Soloviev's influence gradually affected both groups
of combatants. We shall see later on what furious
opposition he encountered from the militant party
when he began his work; but before we consider
these struggles, and his task in the capacity of peace-
maker, we must see how, through the events that
formed his character, Providence prepared him to
understand and help his fellow-countrymen.

CHAPTER III

SOLOVIEV's family surroundings and the social conditions under which his childhood was passed prepared him for the task that lay before him. He grew up during a great crisis of national thought, and his precocious experience enabled him fully to understand the aspirations and sorrows of his people. An early initiation into such matters is dangerous for men of average ability, but most valuable to those of higher intelligence. It prepares them to influence those around them in a manner that may be both very effectual and very opportune.

Vladimir, the second son of Serge Mikhaïlovitch Soloviev, the first and most painstaking Russian historian, was born on January 16, 1853. His father, then thirty-three years of age, had just published the first volumes of the great work that he continued until his death: *The History of Russia from the Most Remote Times* (until 1780). In 1896 Vladimir wrote a touching article in memory of his father, from which we shall derive some personal information. His merits as an historian are summed up by his son in a few eloquent words: " My father had a passionate affection for Orthodoxy, science, and his native land."

On his mother's side Vladimir was connected with the family of the Ukraine philosopher Skovorod. Her name was Polyxène Vladimirovna Romanov, and she survived until June, 1909. Vladimir's grandfather, Mikhaïl Vassilievitch Soloviev, was a priest of the Orthodox Church. The boy was brought up in the principles of primitive Slavophilism until he entered the Gymnasium at Moscow in 1864, when his surroundings underwent a complete change. Although the book had been condemned by the censor, Büchner's *Force and Matter* was being studied enthusiastically by young Russians, and Soloviev secretly read it in German; afterwards he read Strauss, and then Renan's *Vie de Jésus* in French.

As early as 1867 he cast aside Christianity and all faith in the spiritual life, and wrote: " Büchner's catechism of science prevailed over the religious catechism compiled by Philaretus." It was a childish judgment, and its deliberate reversal at a later date revealed a maturity of thought unusual in one so young. Until this change of opinion took place, the boy had no religious convictions. On August 18, 1872, when he was nineteen, he wrote: " At the age of thirteen or fourteen I was a zealous materialist, and puzzled how there could be intelligent people who were at the same time Christians. I accounted for this strange fact by supposing that they were hypocrites, or that there was a kind of madness peculiar to clever men."

This boy of fourteen refused to take part in any religious act, even at home, and regarded this refusal as a point of honour. His father knew him well, and was careful to avoid taking any sudden step in dealing with him; he uttered no reproaches, and only insisted upon the serious nature of the problem of life, urging him to beware of rash decisions. The boy undoubtedly considered all arguments for and against materialism, and yielded at last to objections that had more weight than the unscientific reasoning of men like Büchner and Renan. Thus by taking his son's difficulties seriously, Serge Soloviev delivered him from them.

A strange kind of intellectual precocity occurs sometimes among the Northern nations, and this little Russian of fourteen endured religious agony such as St. Augustine felt before his conversion. Like the great Latin Doctor, to whom he was eventually to owe so much, the young Slav, faced by the two problems regarding matter and the existence of evil, had recourse to a kind of Manichean philosophy, which German pessimists, and especially Schopenhauer, inculcated. He saw further than his fellow-students, who almost all adopted practical materialism and the delights of positivism. They cared little for theories, and were contented to have at hand a few aphorisms, just enough to excuse their conduct. This lack of interest as to the truth shocked Soloviev, who once for all made up his mind to respect truth always and to sacrifice everything to it. His devotion to truth was not unrewarded.

It is worth while to trace the path—a most remarkable one for a child—by which he came back to religion. A mind poisoned by materialism often needs philosophy as an antidote before it can be converted. German sophistry had obscured Soloviev's intellect, so that he had come to accept nothing except on the evidence of his senses, and to recognize nothing as real except matters still incompletely differentiated, and ever tending through world processes to a state of yet more calamitous evil. Where could a remedy be discovered for this malady? He found it in Spinoza, whose works he read at the age of fifteen, and who was to him what Plotinus and the Platonic school had been to St. Augustine. The reality of the spiritual life and the necessary existence of God, that he had recently rejected as absurd hypotheses, now suddenly were seen to be firmly established, and his conversion began. Four years later, on the subject of the " Orthodox materialists of Büchner's school," he writes: " The logical absurdity of their system is apparent, and the more rational materialists have adopted positivism, which is quite another sort of monster, by no means despicable. As to materialism, it has never had anything in common with reason or conscience, and is a fatal product of the logical law which reduces *ad absurdum* the human mind divorced from divine truth."

At the age of nineteen, when he wrote the above words, Soloviev had definitely taken up the study of philosophy. The choice had not been made hastily. On leaving the Gymnasium he had

achieved such success in the faculty of physical
science and mathematics at the University of
Moscow, and seemed to have so great an aptitude
for science, that both professors and students
foretold that he would soon occupy the chair of
palæontology. Suddenly, however, he found that
natural science threw but little light on the mysteries
of human life, and was incapable of consoling,
guiding and saving souls, whilst Russia stood in
such urgent need of consolation, guidance and
salvation. Consequently he abandoned science and
turned to philosophy, not in a dilettante spirit,
but in that of an apostle, for he felt himself called
to an intellectual apostolate, and determined to
study and think, not as a scholar or dreamer, but
in order to help and teach others.

Art, thought, and poetry practised simply for
their own sake filled Soloviev with horror, as being
selfish amusements. He was an artist, a thinker,
and a poet, but always for the sake of others, and
from the beginning of his conversion he made it
his aim to live for others, and to think for the love
of God and the good of souls. Later on he expressed his aims in the graphic phrase: " He will
be saved who has saved others."   But, it may be
asked, was not his conversion attended by more
dangers than his materialistic errors ? Spinoza's
pseudo-divinity is a bottomless abyss, and men of
vigorous intellect have been overwhelmed by the
mysterious fascination of its half-lights, and by the
majesty of its shadows, that are always vague and
uncertain in their logical development. Must not

an attempt to fathom these depths be fraught with peril to a boy as enthusiastic and unbalanced as Soloviev then was ?

No; at the age of sixteen he could resist Spinoza's charm, and perceive and condemn his exclusive apriorism, and, whilst appreciating his master's rigorous method, he asked himself whether it were legitimate in its origin. He had recourse to other teachers, and ere long his philosophical and religious training brought him to accept the transcendent nature of God and His personality. He always retained an appreciation of Spinoza's practical methods, and justified it by his own experience. In 1897 he wrote that " in this period of unintelligent empiricism or narrow criticism, certain formulæ of the Ethics, expounded to an audience consisting of Russian positivists, would effectually rouse them from the slumber of materialism. Contact with the *de Deo* would be a revelation to many minds, and would almost constrain them to adopt the attitude that befits us all in face of the Absolute—viz., the attitude of humility, which is the prelude of every conversion."

During Soloviev's youth, whilst he lapsed into unbelief, and then regained his faith, party spirit increased in Russia, and young men and even children were affected by it. In a town like Moscow no one could ignore or be indifferent to the struggle, and all were forced to range themselves on one side or the other, until practically all educated Russians were divided into two groups of approximately the same size, representing the two lines of thought already described. At first the forces were in equilibrium, but, as the strife continued between the hostile parties, the more violent spirits monopolized the direction of each, as is generally the case in times of crisis. Moderate Slavophiles, such as Kirievsky, Khomiakov, and Aksakov sank into insignificance in comparison with men like Katkov, Strakhov, and Danilevsky, and it was not long before the Sacred Synod passed completely under the oppressive and intolerant sway of Pobedonostsev, its procurator-general.

The same thing happened in the Liberal party, and the years 1862-1864 witnessed both the glories of Katkov, the Neo-Nationalist, and the first triumphs of Tchernitchevsky. Under the latter's leadership a small but noisy section of the Occidentalists adopted revolutionary principles, and claimed to be heard because all Russia supported them. Even the wiser members of the party seemed compromised, and the Slavophiles rejoiced accordingly.

For a time Herzen still continued to rise; afterwards Lavrov, Kropotkine, and Bakounine. Outbreaks of violence occurred, which were sternly put down; and no one could foresee what would follow.

Russia has been profoundly affected by the events of the years 1900-1909, but it has stood firm, and the worst that has happened is trifling in comparison with what might have been anticipated from the mutual misunderstanding of prominent men between 1860 and 1880, when there seemed every probability of the conflict of thought leading to civil war. Had this actually broken out, there can be no doubt that it would have been a war of extermination, so great were the accumulated grievances, the long-repressed enmities, and the needs of personal defence. To intelligent spectators the " executions " in Poland in 1863 appeared to be merely a prelude, a comparatively mild rehearsal, of the great drama in which Russians would fight against Russians. Unknown to the Imperial Government of Russia, the insurrectionary Government of Poland remained in the capital of the kingdom, using the University of Varsovie as its headquarters. Bands of peasants were under the direct command of the students and the indirect control of the professors; and many people expected similar organizations to be formed throughout the Empire. The struggle in Russia would be, they thought, far longer and fiercer than that in Poland, as the field of battle was at once much larger and more subdivided. Enemies would meet face to face on every square mile of the boundless plains; men would engage in countless single combats, and never be able to withdraw into a well entrenched camp; and both sides would display the same endurance, the same quiet enthusiasm, the same passive obedience to their chiefs, the same calm fatalism in face of death, the same mystical devotion to their cause, and the same determination to kill or be killed.

From 1860 to 1880 this civil war was continually on the point of breaking out, and pessimistic observers foretold the approaching disturbance, if not the total destruction, of the Russian Empire before another fifty years had passed.

During fifteen years there was a constant succession of deeds of violence, beginning with Karakozov's attempted assassination of the Tsar in April, 1866, and lasting until the explosion which destroyed part of the Winter Palace, and buried under the ruins a hundred soldiers of the Finland regiment (February 17, 1880). Later still, on March 13, 1881, Alexander II., the Liberator, was assassinated. In discussing these fifteen years, M. Leroy-Beaulieu remarks that twenty or thirty resolute young men, having entered into a compact with death, held in check the Government of the largest Empire in the world. Their audacity found support in a kind of tacit connivance on the part of the nation. The horrible nature of their crimes ought to have roused the masses against them, but the short-sighted severity with which these crimes were punished bestowed a certain amount of prestige upon their perpetrators. Where a few students were guilty, thousands suffered, and where a few officials incurred suspicion, hundreds were dismissed. Hence there was no lack of recruits to the party of malcontents, and many deluded people received an impetus in the direction of revolution, whilst their hasty actions strengthened the extreme party of Orthodox Slavophiles. Thus the irreconcilable differences between the two schools of thought were ever increasing; the gulf between them grew wider and wider, and no one attempted to bridge it over. Each party upheld

a portion of truth, but was so much dazzled by its
brilliancy that they never even attempted to con-
template, as a whole, the jewel to which their fragment belonged. The war-cry of one party was
" the dignity of the individual," that of the other,
" the sanctity of authority." The former failed to
see that their materialism could not account for
this dignity; they overlooked the fact that, where
there is no authority, there is no safeguard for mutual
respect; and, above all, they forgot that men in
authority were still human personalities. The
others laid too much stress upon authority, and their
statements, though fair enough if restricted to the
primary source of power, and the obligation which
makes just laws binding upon men's conscience,
were falsified by their exclusive and absolute
character. They deified those in authority, their
caprices and excesses, and even their contempt for
whatever is not Slavophile.

The assassination of Alexander II. on March 13,
1881, disarmed neither party; he was killed by
one and avenged by the other. Crime is unpro-
ductive, and excessive chastisement effects no
remedy; wounds are not cured by bloodshed.

The malady that infected men's minds remained
undetected, and no one thought of discovering and
teaching what was right. Both parties were
content to thwart by violence every unpleasant
application of ideas held by their opponents. If
this state of mutual exasperation had continued, its
logical consequences would have developed, and the
most trifling event might have brought about a

disaster. For instance, the troubles that followed the war in the East would, if they had occurred a few years earlier, have assumed quite another form. Between 1905 and 1907 the disturbances that took place, and the measures employed to repress them, were mild in comparison with what had been foretold twenty years previously; immense progress had been made since 1880.

No one can, or attempts to, deny that great progress has been made, but what caused it ?

The causes are certainly complex; men were weary of continual acts of violence; they had learnt more, and gained experience; they had come into closer contact with Western Europe, and their dreams had been dispelled by the force of realities. All these things facilitated a better mutual understanding between rulers and ruled, and encouraged those who advocated the adoption of a less hostile attitude towards the Catholic Church. But who taught Russians of the present century to hold broader views ? To their parents the ideas of authority and liberty seemed so fatally antagonistic that there was no possible *via media* between Orthodoxy and unbelief. Yet now it is plain that an agreement can be effected between authority and liberty, if they are well apportioned. Such a reconciliation is necessary and even easy. A man can be at once a scholar and a believer, and the human conscience can resent the stagnation produced by Oriental Orthodoxy without denying Christ; and, finally it is possible to love the Catholic Church without any loss of patriotism.

To what is this transformation due ? We do not
hesitate to ascribe it, to a very large extent, to
Vladimir Soloviev's example, work, and posthumous
influence.

That Soloviev's influence is very great is proved
by the evidence of facts, as well as by written
testimony. Many Russians acknowledge it, and
still more, though they hesitate to confess it, are
affected by it indirectly and almost unconsciously.

It is a remarkable fact that Soloviev had recourse
to no compromises or half-truths in order to effect
a *rapprochement* between the two parties that were
apparently quite irreconcilable. He never thought
of forming a party himself, and consequently all
were disposed to listen to him; and nothing was
further from his intentions than to meddle with
politics, and, by thus holding aloof, he was able to
accomplish more than could have been effected by
ill-timed intervention. Frank independence was
the keynote of his power. He loved truth for its
own sake, and welcomed it wherever he found it.
In so doing he exposed himself to ostracism on one
side and anathemas on the other, but both were
alike to him, if only truth could thus be discovered
more completely and stated in all its fulness.
He desired the whole truth, and abhorred
exclusivisms to such a degree that the very titles
of his books reveal his tendency to exalt the
integrism of truth in opposition to formalism.
He was an integrist, but he was honest; and
although his plain speaking as a moralist offended

all parties at first, his honesty won them over in
the end.

Professor Brückner of Berlin writes as follows of
Soloviev in his *History of Russian Literature :*
" Soloviev, a moralist and theologian, is one of the
most interesting representatives of modern Russia
and its intellectual fermentation. He is fearless
and quite devoid of all self-seeking in his ardent
zeal for making the truth known. . . . In an age
of absolute positivism and indifference to all theories
and metaphysics in general, his great merit has
been to bring back men's attention to⋅ the eternal
problems, to have upheld the great moral principles
in eloquent and poetical language, with the force
of intense conviction, brilliant dialectic, and profound knowledge. This is his great merit, and it
is doubly great in a country whose native literature
is very poor in works on moral philosophy, and
where the people are intellectually so indolent [the
German author is expressing his own opinion] that
they are satisfied with the merest outlines of truth;
for instance, they welcomed positivism between
1860 and 1870 and Marxism in 1890 and the following years."

Soloviev's influence was partially felt for a long
time before it reached its full strength in 1900,
the year of his death, and it still continues to
increase. In 1907 Hoffmann, a competent critic,
wrote : " One of Tolstoï's stoutest opponents in the
department of philosophy and religion is Soloviev,
who has acquired great respect and popularity in
his own country. He has taken up a position

differing from Tolstoï's on two essential points, for he adheres to the historical conception of Christianity and to the Nicæan creed, and rejects the axiom of Tolstoïsm that forbids resistance to evil. No one can read Soloviev's last work, completed only a few days before his death, without indescribable emotion. His historical insight is so profound, so clear, and so penetrating . . . and is plainly the outlook of a believer, a true follower of Him Who said: *Ego et Pater unum sumus.* At this point criticism is silenced, for love begins."

The same note is struck in the *Slovo* of March 13/26, 1909, in an article by Vassili Goloubiev on a lecture given by N. A. Kotliarevsky: " The name of Vladimir Soloviev is becoming more and more popular. No one can begin to read his works without yielding to their charm and loving the author. As a theologian he believed in a personal God and in the truth of Christianity. He made it his aim to reveal the living Christ to our generation, and to prove the reality of the Christian spirit in our modern civilization. He had profound faith in the other life. We accept this belief as a dogmatic formula, but what influence has it upon our daily life ? None at all, and this is the cause of our practical materialism. Now Soloviev, though living in the world, possessed most lively faith, and in this lay his originality. His whole life was ordered so as to testify to his faith in the divinity of Christ, and yet it would be difficult to imagine a more accomplished man of the world than Soloviev. He was to be found wherever there was life; he was keenly interested in every aspect of life, in art and politics, and even in the irrigation of the Steppes. He was not out of touch with the things of earth and his verses are full of human feeling. But at the same time God was always present with him, and he was a Christian in the highest sense. This union between worldliness and spirituality was the great mystery in his character. His life was in keeping with his writings."

Hundreds of similar quotations might be made, from authors differing widely one from the other. They do not prove that Soloviev attracted men of every type. Furious attacks did indeed give place to esteem, and hatred to respect, but a man of such marked personality could not fail to arouse contradiction. The opposition to him died down, but did not disappear, and perhaps it does more than indiscriminate enthusiasm could do to increase his prestige.

Let us see what his antagonists say of him. Merejkovsky and Ossip-Lourié express very clearly their opinions. The former, in a book bearing the title *The Tsar and Revolution*, bears witness to Soloviev's extraordinary influence, which is, from the author's point of view, an additional reason for regretting his attitude. Soloviev had, he says, inspired the Russian nation with his moral teaching; if he had chosen, he could have incited it to revolution, and that he failed to do so is regarded by Merejkovsky as an unpardonable mistake; " he preferred to become a Russian John the Baptist, and to preach obsolete duties in the desert."

Merejkovsky seems to have forgotten that John the
Baptist attracted crowds, in spite of preaching in
the wilderness, and taught as a precursor, not as
one recalling the past. M. Ossip-Lourié's complaints are more varied. He pronounces Soloviev
to be " an extremely shrewd and spiritual dialectician, a scholar, a poet, and an honest thinker,
possessing a thorough knowledge of all the systems
of philosophy." Elsewhere he writes: " In Soloviev
reason and sensation are in perfect equipoise; he is
not an ecstatic, and his mysticism may be described
as the outcome of his reason, rather than of his
inward religious perception." " In his private life
he was an ascetic. . . . As a rule the force of the
religious idea weakens other intellectual states,
but this was not the case with Soloviev, whose
mental activity never flagged during his whole life.
. . . He was neither neurotic nor subject to
hallucinations, but simply contemplative, and a
fine thinker." There was, however, one point on
which Ossip-Lourié differs from Soloviev, and it
redounds more to the latter's credit than all the
praise lavished upon him: " Soloviev thinks that
the salvation of the world will be found in Christianity and in the union of the Churches. This
fact appears strange, for he must undoubtedly
have been aware of their conflicts, and yet it is
certain that in his mind Christianity occupies the
place assigned by Spinoza to Absolute Substance.
We should readily accept Soloviev's opinions if he
did not insist upon the point that the sole aim of
each individual and nation was to participate in

5

the life of the universal Church, each according
to his own particular power and capacity. He
maintains that no union is possible among men
except in God, the principle of union."

Members of the opposite party brought another
charge against Soloviev, and even some of his own
friends share their opinion. They speak of him as
a true Christian, but many stop short at that point,
and feel bound to criticize what they call his Latinism.
Even Radlov expresses some uneasiness on this
subject in his article on Soloviev's mysticism, as
well as in the biographical introduction to his
friend's collected works. It is incorrect to speak
of Soloviev's Latinism, and it would be better to
say that he possessed Catholicity in heart and mind,
or, as Father Aurelio Palmieri puts it, " religious
enthusiasm for the truth and unity of Catholicism."

The accusations brought against him fall into
two classes. The one party objected to him for
holding antirevolutionary and Christian views ;
the other complained that his religious convictions
were too decidedly Catholic, and not sufficiently
nationalist. This explains why he was so violently
attacked by the extremists, whose bigotry and
intolerance we have already discussed. Finally,
however, the spirit of intolerance broke down and
its former champions, recognizing the bad results
of their exclusive policy, listened to arguments
on the other side, and not a few were convinced
of their justice. The miracle worked by Soloviev is
that two antagonistic parties have come to agreement regarding him. They unite in admiring and

praising him, and even go so far as to proclaim him to be "the greatest European philosopher during the last quarter of the nineteenth century, and the creator of the first genuinely Russian system of philosophy." Thus those who once joined in opposing him now agree in extolling him, and this change of opinion marks the extraordinary ascendancy that he has acquired over the Slavs. Palmieri accounts for it as follows: "Soloviev united with his ardent religious enthusiasm wonderful intellectual gifts and extraordinary learning, so that he possessed the most vigorous mind and the most generous heart in modern Russia." Vogüé writes in similar terms of "this *Doctor mirabilis*, one of the most original figures of the last twenty-five years; a strong man, originator of fresh ideas. . . . His vigorous intellect was developed by his encyclopædic reading, his knowledge of every kind of philosophy, natural science, and languages, many of which he spoke perfectly. The inward beauty of his soul was revealed in his features and in his piercing eyes. . . . He was a great man, and thoroughly representative of his race." We shall see the justice of this opinion when we have studied Soloviev's works and character.

CHAPTER IV

SOLOVIEV AS PROFESSOR

SOLOVIEV's life would seem uneventful were it not for the frequent attacks made upon him. It might be interesting to review these attacks in detail, but, owing to the imperfect knowledge possessed by Western nations of Russian affairs, it would be necessary to insert so many explanations that it appears better merely to mention the principal events, with the dates at which they occurred. They will suffice to outline the history of a thinker who was always progressive, though constrained by his very loyalty to go slowly and cautiously. Having done this, we shall be in a position to examine the psychological reasons for his ever-increasing influence.

After his conversion to Christianity, before his twentieth year, Soloviev took up the study of philosophy. We have already seen what course of reading, what lines of thought, and what aims led him to do this. So great was his zeal for work that at the same time he attended lectures on history, philology, physical science, mathematics, and theology. His favourite professors were P. D. Iourkevitch and V. D. Koudriatsev-Platonov, and he consulted the works of all the chief philosophers, both ancient and modern. He read and annotated in their original languages the writings of Plato, Origen, Seneca, St. Augustine, Bacon, Stuart Mill, Descartes, de Bonald, Kant, Schopenhauer, Hegel, Schelling, Tchadaïev, and Khomiakov. He frequently spent entire days and nights in philosophical reflections, thus working out his own personal line of thought from the abundant material at his disposal.

On November 24, 1874, he read his first thesis in Petrograd. It was a critical study, too systematic, perhaps, but very well thought out, of the twofold evolution which caused idealism, as represented by Descartes and Hegel, and empiricism, as represented by Bacon and Mill, to converge in the direction of atheistic positivism, egoistic, revolutionary, and pessimistic in character. This thesis, which was entitled *The Crisis in Western Philosophy*, attracted much attention, and brought Soloviev into contact with a large number of intellectual Russians, who were divided in opinion regarding him. His enthusiastic admirers pronounced him to be an inspired prophet. Bestoujef-Rioumine, a friend, admirer and rival of Serge Soloviev, wrote: " If to-day's hopes are fulfilled in the future, Russia possesses a new genius, who in manner and style resembles his father, although he will surpass him. I have never been conscious of such prodigious intellectual force at the reading of any other thesis."

Opponents soon came forward, for the representatives of philosophy in Russia were at that time all infected with positivism, and the thesis was plainly directed against them, as its secondary title showed. Soloviev replied to the attacks of Lessevitch and Kavelyne, and for a time victory rested with him. A month later, when he was only twenty-one, he was appointed lecturer in philosophy at the University of Moscow, where his first course of lectures on metaphysics and positive science began on January 27, 1875. The young professor's introductory words were characteristic: " In every sphere of activity, man thinks primarily of liberty." This was a bold but seductive statement to make before a class of Russian students, and the closing remark, expressive of a wish rather than an assertion, struck the same note: " Human thought turns instinctively in the right direction, towards what will give breadth and freedom to the knowledge and life of man, and is far from imposing obstacles and restrictions."

This allusion to freedom might be supposed to refer to a relaxation in the severity of the Government, but it really called for changes of quite another kind, and the professor proceeded to develop his argument as follows: The necessities of existence impose upon every man three social obligations, economic to enable him to utilize the material world, political to regulate his relations with his fellow-men, and religious, to put him in due submission to God. Why do we accept these social conditions only under constraint ? Why should philosophy reject them, whilst professing to ameliorate them ? Is man incapable of recognizing in them a providential will, worthy of his voluntary affection? On these arguments Soloviev founded his theory of a free theocracy, by which he meant a deliberate and loving recognition of God's supremacy, in the voluntary acceptance of which true liberty could alone be won.

There was in his theory more asceticism than danger to the Government. At first he was understood, but this was not always the case, and the suspicion of the ruling class led to a series of actions that brought Soloviev's brilliant career to an abrupt end only six years later. It is true that this catastrophe had been foreshadowed more than once by partial disgrace and long periods of suspension, during which he was forbidden to lecture. This severity was the result of the young professor's extraordinary success. From the very beginning of his career he occupied the position which astonished Viscount de Vogüé in 1880, when everyone in Russia was talking about " the *Doctor mirabilis*, who was delighting the students by his eloquence and personal charm." This testimony given by a Frenchman is worth quoting, for he describes vividly what no one else of his nationality had an opportunity of observing. " Soloviev," he says, " occasionally achieved genuine triumphs, when his eloquence won the applause of all his pupils. We used to listen with alarm to his bold words, with much the same sensation as one watches an acrobat on the tight-rope, wondering if any false step would cause his downfall. But no such thing occurred. He knew how to lead his audience

back to the religious ideal, and reassure the strictest
conservatives; he avoided pitfalls with an innate
skill which upset all our opinions, and that in a
country where one can say nothing and everything.
His success was startling though short-lived, for
his lectures were soon suspended."

Triumphs of this kind aroused implacable jealousy
of the young professor, many of whose colleagues,
feeling themselves eclipsed, avenged themselves by
intriguing against him, though they were not at
once successful in suppressing their rival.   In May,
1875, after he had lectured for three months, he was
suspended for the first time under the pretext of
being appointed to take part in a scientific mission
to London and other towns in Western Europe.
His absence lasted fifteen months, and the solitude
to which he was condemned was a great trial to
him, especially as his health was already undermined
by overwork.   For some time he devoted himself
with almost morbid energy to the study of spiritism
and the Cabala.   In a letter addressed to Prince
Tsertelev he explains why he took up this pursuit;
his object was purely scientific and philosophical;
he hoped that fresh light cast by spiritistic
phenomena would be of assistance to him in con-
structive metaphysics; but, he added prudently,
" I have no intention of proclaiming this aloud;
such a proceeding would not help me in attaining
my desired end, and would only get me into
trouble."

Some Russian friends, resident in London, tried
to induce him to take some rest, and Soloviev

readily complied with their wishes and accepted an invitation to spend an evening with them. His stories added greatly to the merriment of the conversation, although they were interrupted by outbursts of nervous laughter, which is often a sign of overwork in men who lead studious lives. Presently he became serious, and protested kindly though energetically against the vulgarity of thought and the life of logical positivists. Suddenly a playful word brought back a smile to his lips, and his animation prevented his remonstrances from giving offence. This style of conversation remained characteristic of him throughout life; he employed it among Anglicans, who are always eager to welcome Christians belonging to the Eastern Churches, since they wish to effect a rapprochement between them and their own Established Church. So great was the fancy that they took to Soloviev that they called him " the Russian Carlyle."

After a few hours of recreation, Soloviev always resumed work with redoubled energy, feeling impelled to make good the time that he had just wasted. If his visit to London had not been cut short, he would probably have broken down completely; but at the beginning of November he set out for Egypt, travelling through France and Italy. It was on this journey that he first met Catholic clergy, though he did not come into close contact with them. His impressions were not unfavourable, for on November 6, 1875, in writing to his mother, he says: " From Chambéry to Turin I travelled with two hundred and fifty priests from Vendée, who were on their way to Rome . . . worthy men, some of them not at all like Jesuits."

Soloviev was anxious to visit the Thebaid, to learn Arabic and to study the popular religions of Egypt. Before the end of November his Bedouin guides had robbed and deserted him, but he was not discouraged and continued his studies until March, 1876. This first journey beyond the boundaries of Russia ended with a month's stay in Italy and a fortnight's visit to Paris. Innumerable plans were floating in his mind, and it was in Paris that he conceived the idea of writing a book on the principles of universal religion, Abbé Guettée to be his chief collaborator. Nothing came of this idea, except the production of *Russia and the Universal Church*, which aroused Guettée's fury against the "Papist" Soloviev.

During his visit to Paris Soloviev called upon Renan, Prince Tsertelev having expressed a wish that led him to do so. As a child he had admired the author of the *Life of Jésus*, but as a man he criticized him severely, and wrote to the prince as follows: " I could not execute your commission except by going to Renan," then, after giving Renan's reply, Soloviev adds: " Perhaps he was not speaking the truth; he gave me the general impression of being a vulgar braggart."

On his return Soloviev thought Russia a very dead-alive country, and, in a letter to his mother written on May 4, he says: " Petrograd takes no interest in important matters. It is only a distant colony, whilst history would seem to be concerned with some place in Atlantis."

On resuming his lectures at Moscow, he met with the same success and the same opposition as before. On February 14, 1877, when he was only twenty-four, he was informed that he was placed temporarily on the retired list. This time the positivists were not his only enemies; they were reinforced by Katkov and the Neo-Slavophile party, whose ostensible reason for attacking Soloviev was that he had spoken in defence of a colleague who had fallen into disgrace. The real reason was probably a sense of uneasiness regarding his opinions.

In 1877 he had formulated his ideas in a lecture on *The Three Forces*. There was nothing revolutionary about his views, but they were not exclusively Slavophile, and this fact was enough to rouse opposition. He maintained that from the beginning the human race had been influenced by three forces—viz., a tendency to social union, a tendency to individualism, and a higher tendency to reverence God in other individuals and societies. Any exclusive development of the first tendency would result in bringing all men to a dead level, to a uniformity equivalent to slavery and death. The unchanging character of Mahometanism is due to this cause, whilst the Western nations are suffering in consequence of having exaggerated the second tendency, and the Slavs of the East will live on, if they carry the third into effect. The essay deserves to be studied. No one can read it without being amazed at the narrow-mindedness of those who could find in it any ground for alarm. The following quotations will give some idea of its spirit.

" In the West each man's energy is isolated, since each claims the right to aim at his own development to the utmost limit, so that suddenly this energy fails and threatens to disappear. . . . The social organism of the West is divided into isolated and mutually hostile sections, which are further sub-divided into their final constituents—viz., distinct personalities. A tendency to individualism has dominated all evolution in the West, from the time when German particularism began to contend with Roman authoritativeness. It was not, however, until the French Revolution that this individualism was regarded and proclaimed as a serious principle. It began by destroying the organic groups perform-ing the vital functions in the State; then it trans-ferred the supreme power to the people; but in the people which had only just become a living body, it took into account only the aggregation of distinct individualities, that were united by one single bond—viz., community of aims and interests. Such a community may exist, but it may also dis-appear. . . . Yet there must be in every society some ideal principle of unity. In the Middle Ages it was supplied by feudal Catholicism; the Revolu-tion abolished this ideal without providing a sub-stitute. Men talked of liberty, but liberty is a mode of action, not an end in itself. I wish to have liberty of action, not to be impeded, but this liberty cannot be the final end of my activity. . . . Now the Revolution, though it gave an absolute importance to the individual elements, limited their activity to the needs of the material order. It denied the principle of devotion to the common good and of personal disinterestedness. . . .

" At the present day one thing is of supreme importance in the West—viz., capital; and money is the only difference between the upper and lower classes. Socialism, the enemy of the middle class, aims at levelling this inequality in the distribution of wealth, but even if it triumphed without producing a neo-proletariate class, even if it succeeded in effecting a fair division of all material goods and an equal enjoyment of all the benefits of civilization, it would still not have solved the problem of the aim of human existence; in fact, it would only have raised the question in an aggravated form; and socialism is no more able to supply an answer to it than is the whole civilization of the West in its present condition.

" We are told that science is to take the place of faith, but with what does empirical science deal ? With facts and phenomena. I ask for an explanation of them, and all that science can do is to subordinate them to other more general facts. . . . Contemporaneous art is a failure; it no longer believes in the ideal, and being content to imitate and not create, it ends in producing a caricature. Without underestimating the progress made in science and economics, we must rise to a higher level. The primordial necessity of the Russian nation is neither to augment its power nor suddenly to develop a wholly exterior form of activity. Our true strength both in our past history and in our mission for the future has been, and must ever be, our being superior to all national egotism, our care not to waste our best energy in lower regions of activity—in a word our faith in the existence of a higher world, towards which we stand in the attitude of submission that befits us. This is the essentially Slav characteristic of the Russian nation. Even the material humiliation of our country would not destroy her spiritual force. . . . Let us therefore awaken in our nation and in ourselves a positive consciousness of this faith. It is the normal result of interior spiritual growth; let us then go on, raising ourselves above the worldly trifles that occupy our hearts, and the would-be scientific arguments that engage our thoughts. When once false gods and idols are expelled from our souls the true God will enter and reign within us."

The Neo-Slavophile party, though it professed to be orthodox, considered that the Empire was endangered by the suggestion of such an ideal. Their jealousy led them to join the positivists in their hostility to Soloviev, and thus they were able to impose silence upon their too eloquent rival.

Some friends of Soloviev's came forward in his defence, and their protests were so far effectual that on March 4 he was offered a seat on the Board of Public Education. This was only a partial reparation, for he was removed from Moscow and cut off from his pupils and admirers, with no opportunity of obtaining new friends. His freedom of speech was not restored to him, and he was still regarded with suspicion. No sooner was he installed at Petrograd under the immediate control of his superiors, than he began to realize what had happened.

At first all went well, and his *Philosophical Principles of Integral Science* appeared in the *Journal of the Ministry of Education* for 1877. In 1878 he was even allowed to deliver a course of lectures in a high school for girls; and his last thesis, *A Critique of the Principles of Exclusivism*, increased his reputation still further, though after this fresh success he had to accept the position of private tutor at the University of Petrograd. Once more he was employed in teaching at the University, but his term of office, although very remarkable, was even shorter than that at Moscow. On November 20, 1880, he delivered his opening lecture on *The Rôle of Philosophy in History*. Sceptics ask, he said, what philosophy has done for the human race during the last 2,500 years. It has raised men above material cares and resisted all exclusivisms, those which absorb man into a Brahma, and those which never rise above man. It has set us free from all the oppression of external force, it has put down all the pseudo-philosophical and degenerate forms of Christianity, and remains the indispensable intermediary between the learning of the material world and the mystical knowledge of God.

Soloviev's *Twelve Lectures on Theandrism* were published about the same time in the *Orthodox Review*. These lectures were most carefully prepared and delivered before an enthusiastic audience. They expressed the deepest thoughts of a philo-

sopher and believer and marked his first unconscious
leaning towards Catholicism. He was certainly unaware that this was the case, for he gave utterance
with serene good faith to many prejudices, that
still stood between him and the light.

Theocracy and theandrism are words of which
Soloviev was very fond, for they expressed two ideas
that seemed to him correlative. Theocracy, as
he understood it, is the result of God's supreme
dominion over the world. If we freely recognize
His rights and authority, we must inevitably desire
Him to control all our actions. This free theocracy
imposes upon every individual certain obligations
towards his fellow-men and towards society as a
whole. This is generally admitted. But why ?
Why ought man to respect his fellow-man ? Why
should beings of the same nature, all equally limited
and equally relative, arrange their points of contact
with one another according to a scale of duties ?
If altruism is to have any right to crush my egotism,
there must be in each man a trace of the Divine,
and some resemblance to the Absolute Infinite, the
Master, must be imprinted on every human soul.
It is He who alone is, the sole Good and also the sole
Being, who must cause me to feel: " All these others
are Mine; all that thou dost for the least of My
creatures, is done to Me. If we are to love God,
whom we see not, we must love our neighbour
whom we see."

All these imperfect manifestations of God in
man, all this arrangement by which God Himself
uses men temporarily as His proxies, and all these

traces of the Creator were in the past merely the
foreshadowings of the great divine revelation.
A day dawned on which the Word, God Himself,
was made Flesh in the womb of a Virgin. Then
these figurative theandrisms ceased, because the
full theandric reality, the Man-God of history,
had come into being.

But this historical realization of the Man-God
had an object. It was not enough for God, the All
Good, to have honoured with the divine union one
single man, a supreme but isolated representative
of the human race. No doubt in Him, as in all
His brethren, abstract humanity was realized, and
through Him this humanity was associated with
the Godhead. But was the real, concrete mass of
mankind to remain cut off from and deprived of
God ? Did not God in His divine design aim at
saving mankind in general, and at uniting all men
with the Godhead ? Yes; all were to be made
divine; all are called to be *consortes divinæ naturæ ;*
and consequently, if the figurative theandrisms
have ceased, the imitative and participating have
begun; and here we have universal theandrism.
It excludes all pantheism, for only the supreme
Head preserves for all eternity the hypostatic
union—" the Man-God is a unique personality."
Jesus Christ alone enjoys, strictly speaking, the
divine sonship; He alone is the Word eternally
begotten, consubstantial with the Father; He alone
receives eternally from the Father, the first and sole
principle, that eternal gift and fecundity that
causes the Spirit, consubstantial with the Father

6

and the Son, to proceed eternally from Him as well as from the Father. Consequently His theandrism is unique. There is also a hierarchical theandrism, for the Head imparts to the members of His body, all in due order, manifestations and measures of His life. Finally there is universal theandrism, inasmuch as God designs each human being to be united and incorporated with Christ, so that Christ may grow in us to His perfect fulness, and we may help Him at the same time to become all things to all men. This is the only absolute destiny for our indestructible personalities, and it alone brings them to the Absolute. To it are subordinated all the relative and finite ends of this world. Economic and civil societies cannot adopt any more honourable and necessary aim than to collaborate in extending the City of God, His Kingdom, called on earth the universal or Catholic Church.

This catholicity was only an abstract conception to Soloviev at that date. He caught glimpses of it as an ideal still non-existent, but destined some day to be realized through the united efforts of believers. He felt that there must be a rapprochement between the East and the West, and dwelt on this point especially in his last lecture. This idea of religious union, then put forward for the first time by Soloviev, gradually came to occupy all his thoughts, but at the time of which we are speaking, he still regarded it with naïve simplicity. " In the twofold historical development of Christianity," he said, " the Eastern Church stands for the divine foundation, the Western for human frailty. Could these two principles be united, they would give birth to a humanity both spiritual and divine, the reality of the universal Church." So much optimism ought to have allayed the suspicions of the Orthodox party, but it did nothing of the kind. The Slavophiles resented any display of interest in the West, though it was to condone its weakness and its rationalism. Moreover, this course of lectures had begun with a statement which, on the lips of a man less thoroughly convinced, might have seemed a challenge. With calm audacity he had brushed aside the nonsense of University positivism and the narrowness of official orthodoxy. " I intend to discuss the truths of positive religion. This subject is foreign to contemporary speculation, and far removed from the interests of contemporary civilization; but these contemporary interests did not exist yesterday and will have passed away to-morrow. I propose to deal with what is of vital importance in every age. I shall refrain from personal attacks upon those who now deny the very principles of religion, as well as upon those who assail the religion of the present day, for they do well to assail it, since it is not what it ought to be."

Four months later, in March, 1881, the antagonism to Soloviev showed itself openly, and this time he was finally debarred from lecturing. The following incident served as an excuse for his removal from the University. He had been giving a course of lectures in the Institute for the higher education of women at Petrograd, and had taken as his subject a criticism of revolutionary principles. Alexander II. was assassinated on March 1/13, 1881, and this event shed a lurid light on Soloviev's subject; but so far from modifying his statements, he actually alluded to contemporary affairs in his lecture of March 13/25. In order to accommodate his vast and increasing audience, the Credit Association in Petrograd had offered him the use of a large hall, where before an excited crowd, holding various opinions, he condemned every act of violence as an evil and a sign of weakness, saying that such acts were justified neither by God nor by the spiritual principle in man, but subordinated right and truth to material force and brute passion, thus enslaving human personality to the tyranny of environment.

No nation ever advanced in the direction of true liberty by revolutionary methods, and no ruler ever diminished the evils in his State by means of capital punishment. The only force worthy of the name is interior, and nothing but virtue, derived from God for the purpose of uniting men in the bond of charity, can effect changes for the better in social conditions and secure a victory over evil. Soloviev went on to condemn, in vigorous language, the perpetrators of the crime that had just been committed; but he did not stop at this point, and proceeded to point out a remedy for the evil that was devastating his country. Indignation against the criminals was, he said, purely negative in character, and something positive was needed to prevent further outrages. The moral and intellectual perversion that would lead the young into a career of crime must be checked, and this could not be effected by repressive measures, which would be again purely negative; such perversion could be prevented only by converting the masses to morality and Christianity.

The lectures in their original form concluded with a few remarks on the necessity of restoring the principles of Christianity, and on the example that the Government ought to set. The exact wording of these remarks is unknown, as hitherto the publication of the text of these lectures has always been forbidden, and only a résumé of them is given in the third volume of Soloviev's works.

It is certain that he was horrified at the number of executions in Russia, and always advocated a revision of the criminal code, the very principles of which were, in his opinion, shameful and immoral. At the close of the lectures in question, he uttered a few words that were perhaps inopportune, but less inexplicable in Russia than they would have been elsewhere, urging the new Tsar to act as a true Christian, by inflicting upon the regicides a punishment that would render their conversion possible, instead of putting them to death.

In this same year, 1881, Dostoïevsky died at the age of sixty-three, leaving unfinished a work of an allegorical nature, entitled *The Karamazov Brothers*. These brothers were three in number; the two elder represented the past Russia of yesterday and the passing Russia of to-day. They are both horrible types, one immoral and the other mentally affected.

The former, Dmitri, was the incarnation of the traditional Slavophile feeling and of Russian barbarism; Ivan, the second brother, preached the necessity of transforming Russia according to Western ideas, lost his faith and fancied himself an Occidental. After drawing these caricatures, Dostoïevsky skilfully sketched the ideal Russian of the future, as his patriotism suggested. This Russian of the morrow was to be the outcome of the highest aspirations of his country in the past, but also, as a child of history, he was to love progress. He was to resist the folly of the Intellectuals, as being the result of perverted morality; he would respect national traditions, but this respect should be strengthened and supplemented by a still higher love, the love of God and humanity. Whoever reads this book will feel that Dostoïevsky no longer needed to look forward to the birth of this Russian of the future. He had already appeared, and was then a young professor, not yet thirty years of age, whose gentleness and extraordinary intellectual gifts had even thus early attracted the attention of all. In Dostoïevsky's romance the name of the third brother is Aliocha, but his readers were well aware that this name stood for that of Soloviev.

When Dostoïevsky died, Soloviev was only twenty-eight; he had counted upon the great influence that his ideas would acquire through his holding the chair of philosophy at the Universities of Petrograd and Moscow. He had desired the position in order to make converts, not for the sake of money, since his private income sufficed for his simple needs. Now at twenty-eight he saw himself finally removed from all contact with the students, whom he loved with apostolic zeal, and who looked up to him as a brother, not much older than themselves, but already famous. Thenceforward Soloviev could never address a public audience in Russia, and for a long time he was admitted only to private societies and the drawing-rooms of his friends. Towards the end of his life, as soon as the restrictions were removed, he was elected a member of several learned societies, and a few months before his death a chair was offered him at the University of Varsovie; but it was too late.

CHAPTER V

SOLOVIEV AS WRITER

BEING thus reduced to silence whilst still full of
zeal, Soloviev devoted himself to writing, and again
encountered violent opposition. The most important passages in his disquisitions were frequently
suppressed by the censor, and more than once he
was subjected to so many restrictions that he was
obliged to have his books printed in Croatia or
even in Paris. He had no desire to have recourse to
such measures, and on November 28 (December 10),
1885, in order to refute the persistent charges brought
against him, he wrote from Moscow a letter inserted
two days afterwards in the *Novoie Vremia* (No. 3864).
In it he says: " I have just written my first article
in a foreign language, addressed to readers beyond
the Russian frontier. It has appeared in the
Katolicki List, under the title *The Church : Oriental
or Catholic ?*"

No book or article printed abroad, and therefore
free from censorship, contained a single word of
disloyalty towards the Tsar. In his first French
pamphlet, *Some Reflections on the Reunion of the
Churches,* Soloviev was so far from displaying the
least bitterness that, when stating what position

88

the patriarchate of the East ought to hold in the Catholic Church after reunion, he wrote: " The superiority, that in the Eastern Church has always belonged and still belongs in Russia to the Orthodox Emperor, would remain intact."

During the years following his disgrace, his labours were incessant, and the prodigious force of his intellect made itself felt. Tavernier remarks of him that he was insatiable in his desire to study and to understand. He applied himself to very various subjects and his powers never seemed to fail, though his modesty and affability continued unchanged. The extent of his knowledge did not prejudice its accuracy, and the wide field of his studies neither overwhelmed nor concealed his personality; he was at once a scholar and a thinker. Philosophy always occupied a prominent position in his works, for he wished to familiarize the Russians with it. Consequently he undertook, or else super-intended, the translation into Russian of ancient and modern works on philosophy, appending to them critical and historical notes; but his own works showed him to be the foremost philosopher of his nation. He translated or annotated Plato's *Dialogues*, Kant's *Prolegomena*, Lange's *History of Materialism*, and Jodl's *History of Ethics*.

The whole of the section on philosophy in Brock-haus-Ephrone's *Encyclopædia* in eighty-six volumes, was entrusted to Soloviev, who collected a band of collaborators, and himself wrote a considerable number of articles, some speculative, on the words *time, love, metaphysics, predetermination, causality,*

free will, and *extension ;* and others historical, on
*Plato, Plotinus, Valentinus and the Valentinians,
Basilides, Manicheans, Kabbala, Duns Scotus,
Nicholas de Cusa, Kant, Hegel, Swedenborg, Maine
de Biran, Joseph de Maistre,* etc.

To various Russian periodicals, especially to
Questions of Philosophy and Psychology, he contributed numerous articles on contemporary writers,
such as Iourkevitch, Grote, Minsk, Prince Troubet-
skoï, Lopatine, Chtcheglov, Tchitcherine, and de
Roberty, in Russia, and Wundt, Nietzsche, Fouillée,
Ribot, Guyau, Spencer, Hellenbach, and Hartmann,
in Western Europe.

His generous impartiality was so well known, that
in 1898 the Philosophic Society of Petrograd,
wishing to celebrate Auguste Comte's centenary,
invited Soloviev to deliver the oration, and consequently for one day the University opened its
doors to him, and before a vast audience he recalled
his former struggles of twenty-five years ago against
positivism. He upheld his opinions regarding Comte
and his teaching, but drew his hearers' attention to
two main points in positivism; Comte saw the
need of raising humanity to the level of the Divine,
and insisted that the living were bound to recognize
the influence of the dead. These two points were
borrowed from Christianity. Comte failed to distinguish them clearly and failed too in applying
them to his conception of the Great Being; but in
spite of his faulty knowledge, I would gladly believe,
said Soloviev, that he was employed by Providence
to detach the minds of his contemporaries from

materialism, and to draw their attention to two essential truths of Christianity—viz., the survival of the dead who are destined to rise again, and the vocation of all men to theandrism—*i.e.*, participation in Divinity.

These ideas recall Soloviev's views in 1880. His metaphysical and moral convictions grew more definite during his religious conversion, which we shall soon have to consider. He never ceased to state them emphatically, and, although, in order to keep in touch with his fellow-countrymen, he imposed upon himself a certain amount of prudent self-restraint, he never lost his simple loyalty. These characteristics may be traced even in his minor works and philosophical articles. The same depth of Christian thought and the same restrained zeal of an apostolic soul, are manifest in 1883, when he criticized Hellenbach's individualism and metaphysical scepticism; in 1891, when he wrote a dissertation on the philosophy of history; in 1893, in an article on telepathy, dealing with the inquiries set on foot by Gurney, Podmore, and Meyer; and in 1894, in a paper on mediums. The same spirit influenced all his writings, whether he was discussing the moral value of certain political and social theories or defending the action of reason and liberty in matters of religion.

Though Soloviev was *par excellence* a philosopher, he had no contempt for art and poetry, and achieved considerable success as a poet. Here, too, he spoke out of the fulness of his heart, and his verses are often compared by Russians with those of Sully-

Prudhomme, whilst in his criticism of art he resembled Brunetière. Both Soloviev and Brunetière
were in touch with positivism, both assumed an
attitude of conviction, but at the same time looked
forward to the Catholic Church, and both were
overtaken by death before people knew whether their
actions were in conformity with their faith.

There is less justification for comparing Soloviev
with Sully-Prudhomme. Their poems have nothing
in common except depth of religious aspirations;
and even after his highest flights, Sully-Prudhomme
falls back into an abyss of doubt, and his cries for
help, which are as a rule individualist, end in
despair or blasphemy. Those of Soloviev, on the
contrary, rise gradually to the light of faith and the
confidence that proceeds from love. If from time
to time he utters cries of anguish, it is because he
sees his brethren too indifferent to follow him to
the height that he has attained. Many of Soloviev's
poems were published under pseudonyms. In
1895 he brought out a second edition of his collected
poems, and he intended to collect his literary articles
in the same way. It is impossible to mention them
all here—he published essays on almost all the
Russian poets and authors of the nineteenth
century—*e.g.*, Fet, Polonsky, Tioutchev, Tolstoï,
Pouchkine, Lermontov, and Dostoïevsky. We shall
have occasion to refer again to three lectures on
the last of these authors, which roused a sensation
in Russia because they tended to justify his universalist and " Roman " opinions. We cannot do
more than mention the titles of Soloviev's chief

works on art and literature—viz., *Beauty in Nature* (1889); *The General Significance of Art, Lyric Poetry* (1890); *First Steps Towards Positive Æstheticism* (1893); *Russian Symbolists* (1895); *The Picturesque* (1897).

During the same period he was engaged upon large works on philosophy, in which he elaborated the ideas outlined in his theses for the degrees of Master and Doctor. The chief of these works is *The Justification of Good*, dedicated in 1897 to the memory of his father and grandfather; a revised edition was published in 1898, Others were left unfinished—viz., *Law and Morality*, which contains a chapter on capital punishment, and *First Principles of Speculative Philosophy*, published 1897-1899 in *Questions on Philosophy and Psychology*.

These treatises and the theses that preceded them deserve full analysis, but they are overshadowed by Soloviev's works on dogmatic and ascetic theology, to which he devoted his chief attention.

In the midst of his multifarious occupations, he never ceased to learn. At the age of thirty, when his name was already on all lips, and his writings were breaking down ancient categories, and compelling men to think for themselves, he determined to study Hebrew, in order that he might read the Old Testament in the original, and make a direct translation of it for the benefit of the Russian Church. With this purpose in view he retired for several months to a monastery in Moscow. However, contact with the past and the study of the prophets did not turn his attention from the present and future. He was keenly interested in all religious questions, in the Jews, Mahometans, Poles, and Staroviertsi or Old Believers; in official Orthodoxy and its organization, dependence, hierarchy, and monks. He eagerly investigated all these subjects, which cause many difficulties in modern Russia. Soloviev's most characteristic writings on the Russian Church and sects are: *The Spiritual Power in Russia* (1881); *Old Believers in the Russian Nation and Society* (1883); *How are we to Awaken the Powers of the Church ?* (1885).

He protested, as the Catholic bishops in Poland have done recently, against the excessive severity of Russian legislation regarding the Jews. On this topic, a serious bone of contention in Russia, he wrote three important works: *Judaism and Christianity* (1884); *Israel Under the New Law* (1885); and *Talmud and Anti-Jewish Polemics* (1886). In the Slav library in Brussels there is a copy of the first of these works, in which Soloviev himself has restored the passages suppressed by the censor. On the Polish question he wrote: *The Entente with Rome and the Moscow Newspapers* (1883); *Arguments Against the Establishment of a National Church in Poland* (1897); as well as various chapters in his larger works. In order to find solutions for the various problems, he had recourse to historical records and ventured to apply the most exalted principles; in discussing the application of his theories, he descended to the sphere of politics, and in all his explanations and discussions he preserved a calm and comprehensive loyalty, which

was destined ere long to raise him to a broader
outlook than that of the Russian Empire or of all
the Slav States collectively.

The Slavophile party, allied with the anti-
Christian Liberals in their antagonism to Soloviev;
accused him of want of patriotism, and thus his
very loyalty at first increased the number of his
foes, although it finally disarmed them and induced
them to put aside their calumnies, when their
victim's heart had long ached under the charge
of want of patriotism. His reply was that he was
inspired by the purest and most devoted patriotism.
" You tell me," he said, " that love of my country
does not take in me the form of idolatry; that is
true. I love Russia, but I perceive the mistakes
that she has made, and condemn her past and present
injustice. I long to see her still greater and more
glorious, but that does not mean more violent or
more domineering. I hope that she will be in future
better governed and more moral, and eventually
more truly Christian, worthy to be called Holy
Russia. I trust that she will care more for doing
God's will than for conquering other nations;
that she may deserve admiration and envy rather
than fear; that she may defend her Tsar, less for
his own sake than for God's; that she may acquire
influence, less by force of arms than by her faith and
charity; in short, I hope that Russia will be great,
because she acts as the apostle of the world, and, by
preaching the universality of Jesus Christ, she
increases His mystical body and glorifies His one
Holy Church—the Catholic Church—which by the

accession of Russia will become more perfectly and visibly Catholic." Soloviev's patriotism did not prevent him from surveying, unhindered by time, space, and national boundaries, the religious life of mankind, which is, alas, only too often in direct opposition to God's designs. If we compare His divine plan of religion with the history of religions, we shall see a drama with a twofold action, older than the world and more universal than the world. It is indeed a spectacle full of interest both for a contemplative philosopher and for a man of action. "We behold the interests of justice, love, and goodness; the interests of individuals and societies, of human souls and of Jesus Christ; in short, the interests of creation as a whole concurring with those of God."

But everywhere these interests, human and divine, encounter opposition. Universal theandrism, the uplifting of men to God, is the aim, but the spirit that would fain attain to it is everywhere thwarted, being weighed down by rebellious matter. According as we live in the West or the East, we speak of positivism or Confucianism, of theosophy or Buddhism, of revolutionary irreligion or superstitious traditions, of the credulous servility resulting from free thought or false ecstasies and frauds. All these are but episodes in the great struggle, and of greater interest than any other is the schism between the Eastern and Western Churches.

Christendom, originally one and undivided, has for eight centuries been rent asunder into two bodies; the kingdom of God torn into two hostile camps, is indeed calculated to arouse feelings of sorrowful amazement. At the age of twenty-five, Soloviev thought that the vital force of both Churches proceeded from Christ, but the waters of eternal life flowed in two antagonistic currents, and the members of Christ's visible body were engaged in bitter warfare. Instead of working together to fertilize the ground that it might produce new Christians, they fought one with the other, using the Bible, the hierarchy and tradition in their conflict. Prayer, the liturgy, the sacraments, and even the Mass, seemed not to be means of offering praise and worship to God so much as occasions of hostility. Bishops were ranged against bishops, councils against councils, saints against saints, and even Church against Church. Surely it was an irony, if not a blasphemy, in spite of all this disorder to invoke Him who prayed that all His followers might be one ! How could a Christian priest, who had just anathematized some sincere worshippers of Christ, read out the words: " By this shall all men know that you are My disciples, if you love one another " ? How could love of a national religion be reconciled with the doctrines of Christ, and jealous race feeling with those of St. Paul ? Was Slavophile orthodoxy compatible with our Divine Master's command to teach all nations, or with the Apostle's statement that now there were neither Jews nor Gentiles, neither Greeks nor barbarians ?

Only a very full and well-grounded theology could solve these formidable antinomies, and

7

therefore Soloviev, without forsaking philosophy, turned his attention to theology. Thenceforth his activity in both departments was simultaneous and converging. For purposes of criticism, we are obliged to distinguish them, but the reader must be careful not to think of Soloviev as at one moment a philosopher, and at another a theologian. During the last twenty years of his life the philosopher, formerly attracted to natural science, devoted himself chiefly to theology, whilst, on the other hand, the theologian retained the clear and logical methods that he had acquired in the course of his previous studies.

CHAPTER VI

SOLOVIEV AS LOGICIAN

In his first thesis, Soloviev showed that he was a philosopher. Of course there are defects in the volume that he finished at the age of twenty. With the impetuosity of youth he expresses extremely dogmatic opinions and rather forced systematizations.

The pages devoted to the history of Western philosophy before Descartes contain more than one inaccuracy, but his overhasty conclusions were re-examined and corrected in subsequent works. There was some exaggeration in representing the Unconscious of Hartmann as the fatal goal towards which the two irreligious tendencies of Western thought, exclusive idealism and exclusive empiricism, converged. Still, on the whole, the thesis itself, and the replies to the attacks that it occasioned, revealed intensely personal and mature thought, in direct contact—rare at that period—with Western philosophy, and a very wide range of intelligent reading.

The forms employed by Soloviev were often original, as for instance was the case with the two syllogisms in which he summed up the historical and logical evolution of empiricism and idealism in modern times. The major premiss of the former would have been borrowed from dogmatism: We think being; the minor from Kant: We never think except only concepts. From these premisses Hegel deduced: Being is therefore a concept.

Bacon furnished the major premiss of the second syllogism: The true essence of things, that which really is, manifests itself to our real experience.

Locke supplied the minor: To our real experience only isolated states of consciousness manifest themselves. And Mill deduced: Isolated states of consciousness are the true essence of things.

This line of reasoning would justify every variety of pragmatism, from the philosophy of the idées-forces to the vaguest voluntarisms of social or merely moral conceptions.

In all Soloviev's works we see this tendency to trace the growth of the systems in which human thought found expression. He liked to discover their remote origin, in order to forecast their development and results. In this characteristic he showed his affinity with the Western philosophers of the nineteenth century, who were concerned with the evolution of species. He realized that Hegel had greatly influenced the minds and systems of his time, and his opponents committed the strange mistake of concluding from Soloviev's words on the subject, that he had himself been a follower of Hegel. As early as 1874 this anti-materialist champion had written: " Hegel ought to be regarded as the father of the most absolute materialism. His metaphysics are to a great extent answerable for every kind of positivism and for the general hostility to every form of metaphysics. Hegel influenced Feuerbach, whose translated works have done much to spread atheism in Russia, and who gave an extraordinary turn to his most disastrous formulæ. Hegel maintained that man was the supreme substance, therefore, says Feuerbach, it is clear that the divinity for man, is not God, but man, and consequently *homo est quod est* (*edit*)—man is what he eats."

But Hegel's influence is responsible for still more outrageous results, as, for instance, in the case of Max Stirner, who extolled egotism, absolute individualism, and fratricidal struggles, embodying all his system in one formula: "I am everything to myself, and I do everything for myself alone." His "divinity" waged war against all the gods—*i.e.*, men—and yielded only to the physical force that was able to crush it. Besides, Feuerbach and Stirner, we may regard as Hegel's legitimate descendants Auguste Comte, John Stuart Mill, Spencer, Schopenhauer and Hartmann.

Such were Soloviev's opinions in 1874, and he often renewed and emphasized them, so that Ossip-Lourié is justified in saying: "It is a mistake to think of Soloviev as a follower of Hegel; he is the very opposite and criticizes Hegel most severely." This remark is perfectly true, and it is difficult to account for the fact that Soloviev was for a long time accused of Hegelianism by his own fellow-country-

men. What can have given rise to this idea ?
Was it due to his quoting Hegel, and ascribing to
him great talents ?   Neither reason seems adequate.
Does any critic take as his master a writer whose
pernicious influence he condemns ?   Is it con-
ceivable that a man of mean intellect could have
done as much as Hegel to increase the prevailing
confusion of thought ?   My own belief is that
Soloviev would never have been suspected of
Hegelianism, if he had been nothing more than a
philosopher.   One day, however, he declared that
faith in an unchanging dogma did not condemn the
human intellect to stagnation, nor suppress the
desire, need, and means of seeing truth more clearly;
far from being a hindrance to intellectual progress,
faith encouraged and even required it.

Soloviev then understood and quoted St.
Augustine's saying: " Value the understanding of
your faith very highly. He who by the right use
of reason begins to understand his faith, is certainly
superior to him who as yet merely desires to understand what he believes. But if he have no such
desire, and thinks that the things, which ought to
be understood, are simply to be believed, he fails
to perceive the utility of faith " (*S. Aug. Epist.*, 120,
c. II.-III., n. 8 *et* 13).

Some members of the Orthodox party were
scandalized at this return to tradition, and their
indignation increased when Soloviev proceeded to
state that, in order to direct this development in
a way compatible with the immutability of the
faith, the infallible Church has surely received from

Christ an appropriate organ, and this infallible expounder of the faith is the successor of St. Peter.

This statement aroused the fury of those who upheld the absolute fixity of Orthodox belief, and they accused Soloviev of being a follower of Hegel, because he admitted the possibility of growth in Christianity, and perceived in the Catholic Church a means of developing Christian truth that the Holy Synod did not possess. Consequently in the eyes of the Orthodox party Catholicism appeared to be contaminated with Hegelianism. The grounds of this accusation were therefore theological rather than philosophical, and Ossip-Lourié was unconsciously influenced by religious prejudice when he wrote that Soloviev, though a theist in his conception of the First Principle, was a pantheist in his ideas regarding the cosmic process.

These charges against Soloviev were groundless, for he believed in Divine Providence, he knew that God calls men to sanctification, and that prayer places them in real communication with God. This is what the Russians call "mysticism." Soloviev's mysticism was essentially Christian, as all his writings show, even those in which he deals with philosophy properly so called.

In the *Philosophical Principles of Integral Science* an ideal system of thought, organization, and action, is offered to humanity, but because it was ideal, Soloviev did not expect its realization, which would be more impossible than that of the marvels of Utopia. Still the ideal ceases to be a chimera as soon as it influences our will for good, and thus promotes real progress. This treatise, in which ideas are presented in disconcerting abundance, resembles a *Discourse on Method*, in which the same investigation is carried on, and the same conclusions drawn, in every department of human activity, the nature and theory of knowledge, its logical and metaphysical value, its psychological conditions and consequences, and its influence upon individual action and every kind of social cohesion.

Whether it be empirical or scientific, knowledge limited to the facts and phenomena of the outward world will be utilitarian, and will promote the material interests of humanity and the economic development of society. If it rises to general ideas, principles, and their logical connection, knowledge becomes philosophy, which enables human reason to rise higher than it did when aided only by the utilitarian knowledge of facts, but if philosophy is content to stop there and refuses all further light, it wastes itself on the merely formal side of ideas and truths and on purely subjective considerations, and men will logically deny the objective value of these ideas as long as they refuse to ask theology whether any absolute being exists, and what it is.

There are in man tendencies corresponding to these three degrees of knowledge In the social order our appetites determine the social relations with a view to increasing labour. A certain " ideal " desire for order establishes a judicial and legal order among the workers, and subordinates the society thus organized to a form of government.

Finally there is a higher craving, that belongs to
the theological order, for an existence that is
absolute and eternal, and this desire tends to unite
men in a religious society.

Sensible activity displays also three degrees; it
may be contented with material enjoyment and
aim at nothing beyond technical progress in trade
to add to its comfort. It ·may encourage the
æsthetic expression of the idea by means of the
fine arts; or it may lend itself to mystical communication with the other world.

Paganism did not distinguish between these
three degrees, and the result was the most tyrannical,
exclusive, and absurd absolutism that the world has
ever seen. All knowledge was subordinated to a
theosophy without foundation, all society was
subject to a theocracy in which the sole deity might
be the caprice of a man like Caligula, and all action
was dominated by a theurgy that led only to mystifi-
cation. Christianity distinguishes clearly what
paganism confounded; the profane cannot be identified with the sacred, nor the city of men with the
City of God. The reign of liberty would begin at
once, if the pagan principle did not seek to avenge
itself by bringing into antagonism things that ought
to be merely distinguished. In the case of knowledge, for instance, Comte vainly describes the
ages of theology, philosophy, and science as in
conflict one with another. Modern sociologists
emphasize the spirit of rivalry which impels the three
categories of social organisms into a warfare not
for supremacy, but for existence; economic power is

coveted and will soon be conquered by socialism;
the power of government is being transformed into
a Byzantine Cæsarism, irresponsible and autocratic;
and in religion there is a tendency to a kind of
papism, that Soloviev detested.

The misfortune is that each of these powers
aspires to solitary dominion, and to crush the other
two by its own force. In reality exclusivism is no
more injurious to one than to the other; it is contrary
to nature, and an alliance ought to be formed
between them, for thus alone can a development,
suited to the dignity of man, be secured both for
the individual and for society. Every man and
every group of men ought to agree willingly to this
alliance, if only they considered the relative value
of the advantages that it would safeguard; then
they would ensure their own liberty through divine
truth : *veritas liberabit eos.* To designate this alliance
in the three departments of human activity, Soloviev
employed the three words used by Plotinus, which
are well adapted to express the supremacy of God,
and are guarded against any pantheistic interpretation by the explicit mention of the human, though
Christian, principle of liberty. *Free theurgy* denotes the deliberate collaboration of an artisan, an
artist and a mystic, inspired by the desire to raise
themselves and their brethren to God. *Free
theocracy* represents the effort of human societies
as a hierarchy; the social organism works only to
facilitate the distinctly human activity of the mind,
and minds mutually aid one another in realizing
the individual and collective divinization that God

Himself proposes as the end of man, both in His Word and in His Church.

Finally, the agreement of science, philosophy, and theology constitutes an intellectual wealth, a fulness of knowledge, that may well be termed a divine wisdom, or in Plotinus' language *free theosophy*. This theosophy has nothing in common with that introduced from India, which Soloviev opposed strenuously. It is an organic synthesis, in which science, philosophy, and theology are distinct, each being an aspect of truth, not its plenitude. The same spirit should co-ordinate the three points of view, in order to preserve for each its integral value. It starts from different data and follows in each case an appropriate method, but whilst distinguishing them, it does not represent them as in conflict. The synthesis of an integral science is possible only on this condition.

After this introduction, Soloviev indicates a twofold manner of regarding philosophy strictly so called. Some, or rather most, of his contemporaries wished philosophy to stand alone and to be concerned solely with theoretic speculation. In this way it becomes simply a system, having no relation to individual or social life, and it leads inevitably to scepticism by way of materialism or idealism, though various forms may be produced by individuals or in the course of history. In an existence where happiness is neither complete nor lasting, the question " What is the aim of life ? " is of supreme importance. We all desire to ascertain the object of our own existence in particular and that of humanity in general. Soloviev discusses and criticizes these various systems of independent philosophy in a few pages that are a masterpiece of concise and logical argument.

The other kind of philosophy may be called integral or theosophical, for it concludes nothing *a priori*, but goes back to the superhuman and super-cosmic essence, to the Essential Truth whose exist-ence is autonomous, absolute, and supremely inde-pendent of our thought as well as of the reality of the outer world. Cartesianism and the deism of Wolf seem to reduce this essence into a kind of abstract principle, but integral philosophy sees in it reality, full of life and thought, " the real source which imparts to the world the shadow of its own reality, and to our thought that which it copies from the Archetype." But such a philosophy does not stop short at fragmentary or exclusive know-ledge. According to it, truth in all its fulness can be appropriated only by an action of the will inspired by love of the Good, and by an uplifting of the feelings towards the Beautiful. This integral philosophy, being free from all exclusivism, is naturally allied with true science, which is empirical without being narrow; it employs a rational analysis of ideas in order thus to distinguish and define realities, and it rises to superhuman realities. This intellectual reflection is what Soloviev calls *mysticism*, in contradistinction to what he terms *mystique*, which is a direct or rather sensible communication with these realities.

In the third part of the same work he discusses

the lines on which logic ought to be organized with regard to this integral philosophy, He distinguishes the material and the formal aspects of knowledge, and analyzes the nature, value, and origin of ideas and intellectual processes, and finally he states how and to what extent Absolute Being can be known. Soloviev's critics would have avoided many errors in their estimate of him, had they read the pages in which he deals with this last subject. The Absolute, he says, does not as absolute fall under our knowledge, for our senses fail to grasp it, nor does our intellect perceive it directly. The abstractions that we devise do not really represent this Being in whom essence and existence are even logically unseparable. Hence the Absolute cannot be known by relative beings unless He reveals Himself to them. We know Him, therefore, by His own action, which causes all relative beings with all their relative essences and existences to tend towards Him. We catch a glimpse of this action in the empirical phenomena of the outer world, and it stands at the beginning, centre, and end of all our thought.

Thus true wisdom recognizes everywhere the presence and action of God, the presence ever active, the action ever present. True wisdom knows that God is perfect unity and at the same time the perfect All; that He is One and All—not in the pantheistic sense, for everything is not God; the sum total of finite beings does not make them one and God. But He is the perfect whole; He possesses such plenitude of being that the addition of the finite cannot

make it more complete; for He in His simplicity
surpasses and contains all finite beings; He *is* in a
fuller sense than they *are*. He is the perfect whole,
because the manifold terms of His action, compared
with the reality of His Being, bear only a faint resemblance to it, and merely seem to exist; " they are
as if they were not." This conception is neither
agnostic nor pantheistic, but truly Christian, based
upon both the Old and the New Testament, and
taught by Christ and His apostles, the Fathers of
the Church, the Doctors of the Middle Ages, Councils,
theologians, and philosophers, in short, by all
whom Soloviev called " theosophic." It should be
remembered that the Russian, who handled so
skilfully these delicate and subtle questions, was
only twenty-four.

Soloviev's *Philosophical Principles of Integral
Science* is one of his most important works. We
have analyzed it at some length, because his subsequent writings and even his language are unintelligible to those who are unfamiliar with it.

It is easy now to understand the significance
of the thesis written for his degree as Doctor of
Philosophy in 1880, *Critique of Exclusive Principles*,
and easy, too, to see why the word *exclusive* has
been substituted for *abstract*, which would be the
literal translation of the original. When Soloviev
speaks of abstract or separate principles, he is referring to that lower form of philosophy which is concerned solely with thought, and not with life in its
serious aspect. He says: " I term abstract or
exclusive principles certain fragmentary ideas de-

tached from truth as a whole, and discussed to the exclusion of all other considerations. Under these conditions they cease to represent the truth, are mutually contradictory, and keep the world in its present state of intellectual dislocation. These exclusive principles are falsified by their very exclusivism; in order to criticize them, we have firstly to determine their proper value, and show, secondly, that they cannot be substituted for integral reality without involving internal contradiction. Our criticism will be an introduction to the study of those positive principles which influence life and conscience, but are in themselves eternal essence in the sole perfect Absolute."

Two forms of exclusive thought are discussed at length—viz , that which confines itself to cataloguing facts in the name of positive empirical science, and that which constructs a purely formal philosophy in the name of reason emptied of all real content and declared actually non-existent. Through Auguste Comte and Hegel this twofold conception has attracted many minds, but it has the fatal defect of making void the world and thought. Thus exclusive science and philosophy lead to doubt and scepticism, that rob them eventually of all objective value and condemn them altogether. With them perish also all systems of ethics that men have tried to base on science or philosophy, apart from religion.

Soloviev proved this fact with accuracy and emphasis. Fifteen years earlier than Brunetière he proclaimed the bankruptcy of all who attempted to establish a new ethical system, empirical or rational, inspired by personal dignity or by devotion to social progress, but still autonomous. In his panegyric of Soloviev, pronounced at the Academy of Science at Petrograd on January 21, 1901, Koni drew particular attention to this priority on the part of the Russian philosopher, and pointed out at the same time that these views do not affect the legitimate development of science and philosophy in their proper spheres. There is no question of denying scientific results, obtained by the research and labour of centuries, nor of destroying philosophy in order to construct, under the name of faith, a blind and ungrounded theology. Any theology that is out of touch with real life, unable to justify its existence or to develop logically, powerless to subject intellect to truth, and still more powerless to subject to it all human life—a theology that would reject all science and philosophy would display the worst features of exclusivism.

In the intellectual and moral order, in thought as well as in action, barriers must be removed, so that the different spheres may be distinguished, but not cut off from one another. Soloviev suggests that the same remark would apply to the creative genius in art, but he postpones the development of this idea, and never had time to revert to it. He dwells rather on the social application of his principles, and says that a certain essential equality exists among all human beings, because each individual ought to represent the absolute. *Sub specie æternitatis* all men may be accounted equal, since all are finite in comparison with the infinite.

Each, however, represents the divine unity in a different way, and this inequality justifies their plurality, as also their relations of mutual love and support. These relations necessitate spontaneous grouping and the formation of particular societies, but at the same time there must be one society that aims at bringing men into direct contact with God; and this is the Universal Church, to which, in accordance with God's design, all mankind should belong.

Every human society must have a government, and in this world the hierarchy cannot be established on a basis of personal worth; but in an ideal state authority would be distributed according to men's ability to promote the economic, political, or religious welfare of society. Even societies ought to recognize a kind of hierarchy among themselves. " A free Church in a free State " is a watchword that we often hear, but no believer can accept it, for in his opinion it destroys the essential hierarchy designed by God, and assigns too low a position to the Church. An unbeliever, however, thinks that it ascribes to her too lofty a position, since she has no right to legal recognition. History confirms the logic of this, and the formula cannot be a principle, at best it is a practical compromise. Church and State, the spiritual and the secular powers, being both based on the will of God and human nature, cannot be mutually destructive, nor can they exist in complete separation. Their true relation is one of

8

free subordination, originating in true love of God
and man, and existing in what Soloviev calls a free
theocracy. He foresaw that people would accuse
him of being a Utopian, and so he forestalled their
objections to his theory, and deliberately began by
discussing the ideal constitution of society. In
Chapter XII. he says that human society is at once
a fact and an ideal. Positivists are contented with
statical sociology, and do not go beyond facts;
but as soon as a sociologist begins to consider
social dynamics, he is in search of an ideal element
contained in facts, and perhaps, in spite of himself,
he develops an ideal sociology, and holds opinions
as to what ought to be the state of affairs in society.
The positivist conception is condemned for yet
another reason; if society is a fact, an organic
reality, as they assume, this reality is made up of
elements capable of perception and thought. The
fact, therefore, is permeated by the idea, which
directs every activity on the part of the elements,
and which, because it directs without being yet
realized, is Ideal, no matter what its nature may be.

This notion of the Ideal may be ridiculed as
Utopian, but nevertheless the Ideal will always
be the precursor of real activity, and it would be
utterly unreasonable to attempt to suppress every
directing idea. Hence, adds Soloviev, it is important
that a philosopher, who studies society, should first
determine its ideal constitution, and make up his
mind what it ought to be. This is why he omitted
for the time being all that did not bear upon
principles; means of application would depend upon

politics. In practice it would be necessary to pay attention to all facts, but, in order to select and arrange suitable measures, a man of action must have a clear conception of the idea.

Soloviev was from that time forward planning a large work on *Christian Politics*, but he never finished it. In 1883 he published seven chapters forming the part in which doctrinal and ecclesiastical matters were discussed. They bore the title: *The Great Debate and Christian Politics*. We shall revert to this work later; other fragments of it appeared from time to time, and those in which the duties of Russia were laid down attracted much attention, and also roused much indignation in some quarters. The positivists laughed at the suggestion of a moral idea in politics; the Neo-Slavophiles might have accepted the principle in order to apply it to other States, but were unwilling that Christianity should impose on Russian politics any obligation to be moderate. Where foreign politics were concerned, they wished national interests to take precedence; and it is easy to understand their religious attitude towards everything that they did not consider orthodox. This " International cannibalism," as Soloviev called it, was repugnant to him, for he felt that what was genuinely to the interest of his country could not be discovered either in evil or in resistance to God's will. It was in accordance with God's design that countries, races, and traditions should exist, but nevertheless He created only one humanity, and subjected it all to one moral code.

The essays, that we have been discussing in this chapter, all appeared before 1883. For about fifteen years Soloviev wrote no important work on pure philosophy; all his attention seemed to be devoted to theology, asceticism, and the history of religion, and only a few occasional articles proved that he had not forsaken philosophy altogether. In 1897 he consented to revise his thesis for the degree of doctor, insisting only upon a clear statement regarding the evolution of his thought. In an appendix headed " Corrigenda " he says: " Twenty years ago I wrote this *Critique of Exclusive Principles* at a time when I was too strongly influenced on points of pure philosophy by Kant and Schopenhauer." Consequently he carefully revised the chapters dealing with Kant's principle of morality.

During the same year some articles by Soloviev appeared in *Questions of Philosophy and Psychology,* the chief philosophical review published in Russia. Amongst them were three chapters intended to be the beginning of a large work on knowledge. The outline of it indicates what this *Justification of Truth* was intended to be. There was to be one dominant idea—viz., to substitute for the classical Γνῶθι σαυτόν some more comprehensive motto which would assert the tendency of mankind to progress, and this Soloviev discovered in St. Augustine's words: *Deus semper idem, noverim me, noverim te.* His ideal was to begin with personal introspection of the *Ego,* and then to rise to Divine truth in its absolute Being, and subsequently to revert to the beings in process of development that God has produced in His own image. Thus we should raise our thoughts from man to God, only to find God again in all His works, and so we should learn to know the Truth: γνῶθι τὴν ἀλήθειαν.

This work on theoretical philosophy was never finished, and we must deeply regret the fact, especially if we judge of its value by referring to *The Justification of Good, Moral Philosophy*, another work written about the same time and on similar lines.

CHAPTER VII

SOLOVIEV AS MORALIST—" THE JUSTIFICATION OF GOOD "

SOLOVIEV wrote a great deal on morals, and almost all his works deal with some aspect of this subject. Whether he was writing as historian, theorist, critic, or philosopher, he continually referred to morals as the manifestation of practical reason. Incidentally he answered many ethical questions, such as the origin of morality, the nature of duty, the existence and limitations of liberty, and the individual and social bearing of our human obligations.

We have already alluded to some of these articles, but their synthesis is worthy of more detailed examination, in which we can proceed on the lines laid down by Soloviev in his *Justification of Good*, an important work containing a summary of his views as a moralist. Nine months only after its first appearance he had to prepare a second edition, in the preface to which he says: " During these nine months I read the whole book through five times, each time making corrections, so that it might express my thought with greater precision; but in spite of my efforts, it is still imperfect. I trust that it will not bring down upon me the reproach: ' Cursed be he that doth the work of the Lord deceitfully.' "

These words, which are intentionally dated December 8, 1898, indicate clearly in what spirit Soloviev undertook this work on philosophy. His method was plain; he wished to induce his readers to investigate and recognize the reason of their existence and the meaning of life. With this purpose in view, he asked three questions, the first being naturally that at which Mallock stops short: " Is there any justification for life ? Is it worth living ?" The second is: " Must this meaning of life be sought in what is called the moral order ? Man's activity may be animal or properly human; does the higher flight of the spiritual allow or require the sacrifice of what would be excess in physiological tendencies ?" Ollé-Laprune was engaged in analyzing the same problem—what constitutes the value of life for man ? It is closely connected with another question: Whence proceeds the meaning, the significance of life ?

The third point discussed by Soloviev is one more frequently overlooked by contemporary thinkers, yet it is identical with that which presents itself sooner or later to every individual—viz., " What is the aim of my life ? The direction of our voyage or its point of departure should be enough to determine what life is, and what it ought to be, in its integral growth and development."

The rest of this preface has the charm of a fragment of Bourdaloue, although it is difficult to give any idea of this in a brief résumé. Soloviev continues: " How can human activity be displayed, while the mind does not reflect upon these guiding principles ? It is an honour to our generation to have gone below the surface at which the so-called thinkers of the last two centuries stopped short; but the incoherence of the answers to this question flatters the selfish interests of dilettanti. Many have cast aside all religious truth under the pretext of securing intellectual freedom, whereas they are really enslaving their intellect to servile mimicry. They fit into every kind of surroundings, provided that two conditions are fulfilled; their selfish indolence must be left untouched, and it must be cloaked and decked out with many subtle and æsthetic arguments. Some people are induced by pessimism to enjoy life and indulge their caprices. The mind solemnly proclaims that evil is aggravated when perpetrated by one of higher status. There- fore they do not imitate those whose convictions lead them to suicide, but quietly yield to matter, and abandon every supra-instinctive element in life. Are they indeed persuaded that life has no meaning ? Certainly not; they perceive its meaning clearly, but their own life fails to satisfy them, and their cowardice deters them from any effort to raise it. In their fury or despair they resolve to forget, no matter at what cost, and refuse to reflect at all. The life-history of innumerable people at the present day might be summed up thus. Very many others try to avoid reflection by following attractive but barren lines of thought. These are æsthetes, to whom life has a meaning, because it possesses

force, dignity, and beauty, but they desire it to be
independent of all moral goodness, for this imposes
restraints upon them, whereas they are seduced
by beauty, and intoxicated by splendour and power.
Beauty, splendour, and power make up the trinity
which Nietzsche proposed to substitute for that
of Christianity, when he said: ' Slaves may adore
a God who became man and humbled Himself,
but the strong refuse to adore anything except
their own elevation towards the superman; in other
words, the infinite advancement of human beauty,
human grandeur, and human power.'

" How can we talk of infinite advancement ?   In
the eyes of these æsthetes beauty, grandeur, and
power constitute the whole of man, and they end
in the grave—what beauty is there in a corpse ?
In the ancient world Alexander of Macedon combined power, beauty, and grandeur, and yet of
him, as of every other human being, it could be said :
' He fell down upon his bed, and knew that he should
die.'   He was the invincible incarnation of power,
magnificence, and beauty, and yet he died, and left
nothing but a form devoid of all these qualities.
Can any power be worthy of the name that cannot
resist death ?

" Nietzsche was the impassioned preacher of the
body, the real self, the sense of earth; and cursed
those who despised it—viz., Christ and the pariahs
who worship Him.   Nietzsche himself adored
nothing but bodily beauty and strength, idols
which can save neither themselves nor their adorers.
He failed to see that real beauty, majesty, and

strength are inseparable from the absolute Good, and can belong to a creature subject to death only in so far as they are communicated to him by and in this absolute Good. Nietzsche did not notice that the Gospel was not a message of death or mourning, but the revelation of true salvation, joy, and light. Christianity, far from being founded on death, is based upon ' the Firstborn among the dead,' and our risen Lord, whose example is the guarantee of His promise, offers life everlasting to all His followers. Is this a religion of outcasts, slaves, and pariahs ? Do death and resurrection affect only certain classes ? Are Nietzsche and his supermen not liable to death ? Before condemning the Christian doctrine of equality, he would have to abolish the equality of all men in death. If all have need of salvation, how can the religion which alone can save men be the religion of slaves ?

" Christianity is a foe neither to beauty nor to strength; it only refuses to recognize strength in a weak mortal drawing near to death, or beauty in a corpse undergoing decay. Phantoms of strength and beauty, which are in reality powerless and hideous, impose fetters on man, but Christ has delivered us from this yoke, and every true Christian comes to Him, the Source of all that is indeed strong and beautiful. He rejoices with the first soul filled with the spirit of Christianity: ' My soul doth magnify the Lord, the Lord of my salvation; for He hath done great things in me, and He is mighty; He hath revealed His power, and hath raised the humble.'

" No one worships what is weak and hideous, but all desire to adore what is strong, great, and beautiful. Unhappily many devise for themselves some vague chimera of strength, greatness, and beauty, and rest content with their own imaginations. Others seek for real strength and beauty, and find at length that they are always identical with the Good, whose eternal existence robs His worshippers of all fear of death. They do not, indeed, look for definite victory in this life, but expect it with assurance in the future. The former fancy that they will invariably triumph in this world, and their error exposes them to frequent defeats; they fail to grasp the present, and their divinity dies whenever death carries off one of their number; it lies buried in every cemetery."

These stirring passages indicate the scope of the whole work; yet Soloviev had no desire to act as censor. " My intention," he writes, " is not to preach; I do not purpose to teach virtue or rebuke vice. For a plain mortal like myself, such a design would not merely be futile, but it would be immoral, since it would involve an arrogant and unjustifiable claim to be better than my neighbours. My object is not to condemn the accidental errors, however great they may be, which cause men to stray from the right path, but I wish to remind my readers that to every man is offered a choice, to be made once for all, between two courses involving morals; a choice which ought to be made with full knowledge and insight, and which cannot be avoided. Many would prefer not to make it, and desire to find a middle course, not altogether bad, but yet not the way of the Good; a commonplace and natural sort of course, along which men and beasts can saunter. Such is the ideal of which many men dream, and they are quite content to accept the German saying *Allen Tieren fatal ist zu crepieren* (Every animal is fated to die), if only they may previously experience the truth of another similar proverb: *Jedes Tierchen hat sein Plaisirchen"* (Every animal has his own little enjoyment).

"Such a dream is, however, impossible; animals have no choice, and follow passively the way of empiricism; but man must choose; he must arrive at a personal decision, formed by his elective activity, before he can follow the path of moral passivity. If he claims then to be walking in company with brutes, he lies, for deliberate animalism involves a contradiction in terms. No one decides in favour of apathy except by choosing one of the two courses open to human beings—*i.e.*, by deliberately preferring evil through prejudice against the Good.

"To prevent such prejudice, I desire to show the Good as it really is—viz., as the way of life, the one way that is just and safe for all and in every respect. One thing only is necessary if this path is to lead us to our goal, and that is, that we should choose it. It will lead us to Him who is Good in His essence, for it proceeds from Him. He alone is justified in all His acts and justifies our faith in Him. Even before an open coffin, when any other kind of reflection would be out of place, man can utter words of confidence that are the expression of his wisdom, and say: ' Blessed art Thou, O Lord; Thy works declare Thy goodness, and will declare it for ever.'

" For its own sake, human life ought to be directed according to this absolute Good. The life of the individual, the life of society and nations, and the historical life of humanity are three spheres in which God justifies Himself in ways of goodness and justice—but all His loving dealings with man are overlooked by the egoist, who refuses to make any sacrifice or any return of love to God. Even if we have chosen the better path, the necessary stages sometimes seem inexplicable, and one who has knowingly chosen the worse must find them wholly incomprehensible. He will inevitably condemn them as useless and vexatious, and will resent every reminder of God, since it suggests that he has made a bad choice. Nevertheless the light that suddenly flashes in the depth of his soul, and un- expectedly reveals to his conscience the evil of the path that he has chosen and followed hitherto, is only another justification of God's goodness."

Three parts of the book are devoted to working out this design. In the first all traces of good in man are investigated with the precision of our psychological methods. After triumphantly ex- posing the errors of pessimism, Soloviev proceeds to discover the philosophical foundations of morality in the basis of moral action. He sees in human activity three orientations that he approves as good; these are: (1) a tendency and ability to rule

over matter, even the matter which constitutes
our own bodies; (2) the certainty of our solidarity
as human beings; and (3) the recognition of our
mysterious and inevitable subjection to what is
superhuman.

The need of controlling matter in ourselves is
manifested first by the feeling of shame. Though
slow of growth and often very slightly developed,
and frequently cast aside altogether by the will,
the sense of shame nevertheless marks in every
man the first conscious working of his reason; his
mind, hitherto under the sway of matter, asserts its
superiority, and seeks in its turn to rule. This
effort of the spirit to subjugate the body is the
principle underlying asceticism, which weakens the
flesh to strengthen the spirit. The body is a rebellious slave wishing to reign supreme, having to
be subdued, for its duty is to be a helper, not a
tyrant. Its functions may vary, and it may become
a criminal, but in Christianity it rises gradually to
the angelic virtue of perfect chastity. Let him who
can, understand this, said Jesus Christ.

The mutual interdependence that binds men
together is both a fact and a necessity. It would
be criminal to lead a life from which all altruism
and compassion were banished. Asceticism arrived
at the negative conclusion: "Love not the world,
and put aside its threefold attractions." But
simple and honest hearts prefer another rule that
is positive and more exalted: "Love thy neighbour
as thyself." Devotion and brotherly love are
sometimes such conspicuous characteristics of a

man that no one refuses to call him good, and even pessimists recognize his goodness, although they may be ready to crucify him in anger at their defeat.

A student who studies human psychology more deeply cannot fail to perceive that every man by some mysterious instinct knows himself to be subjected to what is superhuman. Education, thoughtlessness, or worldly cares sometimes obscure this fact, which lies at the root of all morality, but if only a breath of wind disperse the clouds, if only one man be true to his mission, the cornerstone is revealed, and all acknowledge that upon it their morality must be based, and this morality will be logical and true, because it is religious. This statement will be proved in the second part.

Psychology has not accomplished its whole task when it has pointed out in man three natural elements of morality—viz., a tendency to asceticism, a tendency to charity, and a tendency to submit to the superhuman. It proceeds to study the action of these tendencies and the development resulting from their being brought into activity; and it is remarkable that man spontaneously describes them as " good." This consideration leads us on to the idea of " better," the conception of something absolutely desirable, which should refer not to the individual, nor to his well-being, nor to his reputation, nor to his activity, and which should not be sought on account of its connection with what is socially good. It is simply *better*, desirable in and for itself. Such conceptions are difficult to put into words, because

they raise our thoughts to something higher, and
are inspired by experience and spontaneously
worked out by the mind. They lead us to assume
the existence of and to desire an Absolute Good,
which is infinitely desirable, and here we have the
idea of God.

This is the culminating point reached by psychology, for the study of its objective value belongs
to metaphysics. Before passing on to this higher
level, we shall each of us do well to look back on
facts that have come under our own observation.
They will suffice to condemn every kind of practical
philosophy that aims at imposing itself upon the
human intellect, without justifying its existence
by definite rational principles. No Eudæmonism
and no utilitarianism can satisfy our aspirations,
for they are powerless to influence our conduct.
An impartial study of human psychology forces
every honest thinker to recognize a rule of morality,
anterior and superior to the impulses of caprice,
and this rule proclaims the existence of duty.

What is the origin of duty ? The second part
establishes the identity of the Absolute Good with
God, really existent. Thus duty cannot depend
upon Kant's postulates, and can be imposed only
by the Infinite. The human conscience is the
mouthpiece of the will of this Infinite Being, although
it may be so unconsciously; but morality, which is
fidelity to the voice of conscience, leads men step
by step towards God. The effort to do right gives
freedom to the spirit and prepares it for devotion,
which in its turn destroys self-complacency, and

by means of this victory over self-will, inclines man to recognize personally, to adore and to love Him who is infinitely good.

Man might, however, still be hindered by want of experience, if he could not keep in view a model of this moral perfection, and consequently the infinitely good God offered him the Divine personality of Christ, whose human body, raised on the cross at the culminating point of human history, displayed the triumph of asceticism, of devoted love for mankind, and of worship of God. This is why every upright soul must choose Jesus Christ, the Son of Mary, to be the guide of his conscience and the example of his life, before he recognizes God in this perfect Man, and before he even professes himself a Christian.

Only a few pages in the *Justification of Good* are devoted to this moral influence of Jesus Christ; Soloviev was right in thus condensing his arguments, for he wished to confine himself strictly to philosophy. Elsewhere he described most accurately what Jesus Christ ought to be to every Christian conscience, but in this work he felt bound to write with more reserve, and perhaps his very conciseness renders his argument more trenchant.

In conclusion, Soloviev proceeded to discuss morals; he did not attempt to determine duties in detail, for each man's conscience must exert itself to recognize God's way in the infinite complexity of our conditions of life. Soloviev tried to discover the principles that ought to guide our conscience in the continual conflict between apparently

9

opposing duties. He dealt with this subject in
the third part at considerable length, and devoted
ten chapters to studying " the action of the Good
throughout the history of mankind." This secondary title suggests a line of thought dear to St.
Augustine; it might seem pretentious, had it not
been intended to indicate the simultaneous existence of the historical and speculative points of
view.

After classifying the rights and mutual obligations of individuals and societies, with their foundations and limitations, Soloviev discusses fully the
historical influences that have shed a progressive
light upon these principles. He arrives at this
conclusion: " The great epochs in which a consciousness of individual responsibility and social obligations became precise, and the schools of philosophy
that exalted either moral subjectivity or the prerogatives of social organisms, all concur in displaying
the great harmony of Christianity, which is more
elastic and more comprehensive in its doctrines
than all its distorted substitutes, since it has effected
a genuine transformation of history, and is the
one absolute rule of conduct; absolute when teaching,
absolute when promising, and absolute when
commanding."

The same synthetical power is brought to bear
upon each of the following questions: How does
ethical teaching decide the national question, or,
in other words, the relation between nationalism
and universalism ? How does it regard the problem
of crime and its repression ? What are its decisions

on economics ? What mutual relations does it
impose on public right, legislation, and morality ?
What justification and what limitation does it
assign to international warfare ?

This important work on the *Justification of Good*
concludes with a long and beautiful chapter on
the ideal, the " perfect organization of integral
humanity," that would be realized, if ethical teaching were freely put into practice by mankind.

Soloviev was too clear-sighted and too shrewd a
theologian to imagine that such a realization was
possible. He had no hope of a sudden transformation of the world, and he was quite aware that no
change would result in the perfection which he desired. But individuals and societies are capable
of improvement, and it is always worth while to
aim at it.

" In the present state of human consciousness
there is peculiar need for men to exert themselves.
Those who have discovered for themselves a satis-
factory and definite solution of the moral problem,
ought to justify this solution for the sake of others.
When the mind has triumphed over its own doubts,
the heart is not rendered indifferent to the errors
of others." One of the chief attractions of truth
is its integrity; it is incomparably beautiful and
persuasive, as long as it is not mutilated by the
rivalry of human passion. Hence it is most ex-
pedient to show men the ideal, the thesis. There is
however, another advantage derived from so doing:
with the best will in the world, no end is ever attain-
able unless it is clearly defined. We must therefore

study incessantly and reveal plainly God's design for human liberties. Thus our approximations, though very faulty, will nevertheless bring about a real improvement.

These considerations justify several pages in Soloviev's work that at first sight might seem purely Utopian. They should be borne in mind by the reader, and especially by any Western theologian, who comes in contact for the first time with Soloviev's religious writings, for they explain the attributes that he is fond of ascribing, in an almost ideal world, to the three visible representatives of God's power.

The Pontiff, the supreme guardian of Divine truth with its spiritual fruitfulness, the centre and highest point of the Christian priesthood, the common father of the visible Church at every moment of her historical existence, represents God in the sight of mankind in general, who, in accordance with His design, may be identified with the Church. The Pontiff's mission is to produce in each soul the person of Jesus Christ, so that this one invisible Head of human society may acquire in that soul the fulness of His mystical body.

A second task is assigned to the ruler of each Christian State, "to the imperial element of Christian theocracy." It is a task subordinate to the first; and must not be absorbed by, nor confused with, nor separated from it. The ruler's task is to organize the social and political order according to the truth of religious principles. It is not necessarily universal, but, being limited to national boundaries, is destined to produce the practical conditions and external means of development both for individuals and societies, so that they may attain to their full worth as men with a view to becoming more and more like God.

" Christ's priesthood is perpetuated in and by the Sovereign Pontiff; His kingship is delegated to the rulers of various States. Finally, His sanctity and the extraordinary graces of His humanity are the object of a third mission. From time to time God chooses certain men, and fills them with His spirit for the salvation of their brethren. In word or deed they are true prophets. Being subject to the twofold authority of pontiffs and sovereigns, they are sometimes constrained to rebuke and condemn the very men who are pontiffs or sovereigns. They are bound to God by the hierarchical Church of Jesus Christ, and are placed by Him in a civil society, so that they have no right to refuse lawful subordination; on the other hand, as their mission is at stake, they must not behave like dumb dogs."

Supposing that, throughout the world, the universal Pontiff, the supreme ruler of each State, and the prophet divinely chosen co-operate, and each in his proper sphere collaborates with the others, how rapid will be the advance of mankind ! " What is good from the economic, the social, the moral, and the religious points of view would thrive together, and men, grouped at last in a Church that was literally universal, would accomplish God's design. In the future all would attain to the plenitude of being that God intended them to possess, the mysterious individual and collective divinization that He promises to the creatures that He made out of nothing, in order to fashion them to His own likeness."

Considerations of this kind were most attractive to Soloviev, but they carry us beyond the domain of philosophy, strictly so-called. In the conscience of our contemporaries, still impregnated with Christianity and influenced by grace, psychology can trace the germs of these high thoughts and some tendency on the part of the soul to rise above the level of mankind. But the precise notion, the reasonable hope and practical realization of this divinization, are beyond the scope of our natural sciences; only a divine communication can make them accessible to us.

" This communication, desired by God, opens to our minds a new sphere of study and contemplation; the innermost depths of the Godhead become accessible to theology and mysticism."

When Soloviev published his *Justification of Good*, he had for twenty years been studying theology; it is therefore not surprising that his philosophical work tended to direct his readers' attention towards his favourite pursuit.

We are now confronted by the question: " To what conclusions did his religious investigations, being perfectly sincere, lead him ?" We shall make this the chief point in dealing with his theological works.

CHAPTER VIII

THE BEGINNING OF SOLOVIEV'S WORK AS A
THEOLOGIAN : "EARLY ESSAYS " — " THE
GREAT DEBATE "—" JUDAISM AND CHRIS-
TIANITY "

In Chapter V. we saw what painful problems
caused Soloviev to turn his attention to theology.
His anxiety regarding religion betrayed itself even
in his earliest works; their author evidently desired
to follow God and to bring others to Him, but
he had not yet discovered with certainty what
path to take. His essay entitled *The Three Forces*,
published in 1877, and others on *Universal Theandrism*, that appeared between 1877 and 1881, all
show plainly that his aim was to promote in the
world the designs of Jesus Christ. This motive
underlay all his efforts to the end of his life, and it
may be defined as a desire to assist Christ in the
task of rendering mankind in general divine.
The means of attaining this end were left vague,
or rather, Soloviev, being still under the influence
of his early Slavophile impressions, thought that
the restoration of Christianity in the world was
a task assigned to Russia and the Orthodox
Church.

He did not deny the merits of Rome in the past, but took it for granted that the Western Church had now fallen into decay. In the theandric Person of Jesus Christ, as well as in His mystical body, the West seemed to see and revere only the human, material, and outward element. At a very early date it yielded to the temptation to enforce belief by violence, and this evil had continued to grow. From the time of St. Anselm onward, a legal fiction had been gradually taking the place of faith in the Roman Church. Love of Christ had been regarded as unnecessary and the ecclesiastical supremacy was all that was needed.

Against this brute forcefulness that professed to be religious, the Reformers raised their protest; but, being themselves infected with the Western poison and by individualism, they produced merely a human work, which finally led to unbelief. Protestant influence, whether rationalistic, Hegelian, or materialistic, became a scourge to Christianity.

According to Russian prejudices, which Soloviev accepted in his early essays, Romanism had continued to decay until at length it fell a prey to Jesuitism, and, having thus reached the climax of misfortune, it lost every Christian virtue; the papal supremacy and the material authority of the Church took the place of everything else.

This idea of Romanism is current in the East, and with all good faith Soloviev confirmed it by a personal anecdote. He stated that in Paris a French Jesuit had, in his presence, denied the possibility of still accepting the dogmas of Christianity, and especially the Divinity of Jesus Christ, but nevertheless, " in the name of civilization and in the interest of the human race," he still required the world to submit to the Catholic Church. Soloviev's honesty is above suspicion, but in 1880 he still employed the name " Jesuit " in the usual Russian manner, as designating any member of the Catholic clergy or of a religious congregation.*

Before 1886 Soloviev was not acquainted with any real Jesuit; the first members of the Society of Jesus with whom he had any intercourse were the Fathers Gagarin, Martinov, and Pierling. He soon became their friend, and the correspondence that passed between them shows how great a place our Lord and Saviour Jesus Christ occupied in their minds and hearts. No member of the Society of Jesus was responsible for the blasphemy recorded in Soloviev's last lecture on Theandrism.

Soloviev himself was aware of the mistake, and he never knew the name of the priest who made the remark to him. Before 1880 he had been in Paris twice, but had come into contact with Catholic priests only through Vladimir Guettée. This unhappy apostate, subsidized by the Holy Synod, had been enthusiastically extolled by a semi-official section of the Orthodox press. Soloviev was destined soon to know him better and to ascertain his lax morality. Guettée's hatred of the Roman Church was so intense that every means of bringing

* The Russian code sanctions this misuse. In vol. ix., article 459, ed. 1899, we read: " Jesuits of all orders are forbidden to enter Russia under any pretext."

it into disrepute seemed permissible, and his hostility to the Catholic clergy knew no bounds, for he had deserted its ranks by a pretended marriage as well as by apostasy. Such a man would shrink from no trickery, however base, if only he could implant anti-Roman prejudices in the mind of a man like Soloviev.

In any case, if at first Soloviev was taken in by his fraudulent device, it could not long hold its ground against truth and experience, and very soon Guettée hurled maledictions upon the " Jesuitism " of this Russian, who became " more popish than Bellarmine."

Anti - Roman prejudices, such as we have mentioned, were universally accepted as true in Russia. Honest believers knew the Western Church chiefly from four series of documents—viz., Protestant compilations published in Germany, anticlerical pamphlets from France, the " traditions " of Constantinople, and the national controversy on the Polish question.

Loyal souls may well be misled by such a consensus of false reports, and their complaints, often most extraordinary, keep alive prejudices that seem ridiculous to a reader who knows their wish to be honest. For instance, Alexis Stephanovitch Khomiakov, a man of generous nature, ardently desired the reunion of the Eastern and Western Churches, and laboured to effect it between 1840 and 1860. Yet he uses with full conviction phrases such as: " Romanism is only the oldest form of Protestantism," and elsewhere he makes a remark, that is

more startling in the East, where for centuries the
idea of national churches has prevailed: " Romanism
is nothing but separatism . . . do not shut your
eyes to the fact; the separatism of the Western
Roman Church is evident, and is the one formidable
scourge for humanity."*

Now Khomiakov was a wise and honest man,
whom many Russians suspected of excessive sympathy with Rome. The more moderate party
derived their knowledge of Catholicism from his
works, and Soloviev at first did the same. This
fact is enough to account for his contempt of
Romanism as the " implacable foe of all progress
both intellectual and social, disdaining and destroying all personal dignity." In spite of the violence
of his opinions, a certain amount of reserve shown
with regard to traditional prejudices exposed Soloviev even then to the hostility of the extreme
Slavophile party.

It was necessary to recall these original prejudices
and the influence of his Orthodox surroundings,
in order to appreciate the distance traversed by

Le ters to Archdeacon Palmer. William Palmer,
fellow of Magdalen College, Oxford, was in 1840 commissioned
by the Anglican Bishops to go to Russia, in order to study
the means of forming an Anglo-Russian Church. He wrote
several books on the subject of his travels, interviews, and
plans. His study and experience gradually convinced him
that the Roman Catholic Church was the Church of divine
origin, and he became a convert some years before his death.
He never lost interest in the religious future of Russia. His
valuable library, bequeathed to Fathers Gagarin and
Martinov, is one of the treasures of the Slav Library in
Brussels.

Soloviev and his courage in assuming another intellectual attitude, in the face of his fellow-countrymen.

Certain facts caused him to doubt the justice of the Russian national antipathy to Rome, and, although his time was fully occupied with his philosophical work, he resolved to find out the truth. The task seemed likely to be overwhelming, but, if his efforts were to be rewarded with the truth, the labour involved was nothing to Soloviev. He devoted himself heart and soul to the work, in which a comparatively small part was played by handbooks dealing with the Eastern and Western Churches. He preferred to study the great authors and their works at first hand.

He read the Acts of the Councils in Mansi's folio edition, and studied history and tradition in Migne's Greek and Latin patrologies. The abundant notes that he took gave rise to a number of very personal articles on the Fathers of the Church. His favourite authors were St. Justin, St. Irenæus, Origen, the two St. Cyrils, St. Gregory the Theologian, St. John Chrysostom, St. John Damascene, and among the Latin Fathers he highly esteemed, next to St. Augustine, Tertullian, St. Cyprian, and St. Gregory the Great. This list is not exhaustive.

After the discovery of the *Didache*, he studied it so carefully that he was asked to publish his Russian translation of this precious record of the first century of Christianity. The introduction to it is worthy of notice. In it he points out that this document shows how, from the earliest time of Christianity,

Providence has always coupled with the perpetuity of the hierarchy, of dogma, and of the sacraments a possibility of development in their outward manifestation. The Orthodox Church makes of this process in the Catholic Church a charge of innovation.

It is not surprising that this essay roused much hostile criticism, but Soloviev was not unprepared for it; in fact, he had foreseen it from the time when he began to revise his works on history and dogma, and in spite of all opposition he continued his revision most conscientiously. Byzantinism, being antagonistic to everything Roman, has spread rumours, more or less fanciful, all over the East; and Russia, so long isolated from other nations, continues to propagate this jealous hostility. Soloviev investigated all the strange ideas current on the subject of Western Christianity; they were not all unreasonable, and some, though false, could be explained as plausible. Many real faults inevitably occur in every human society, and even among the representatives of divine truth. Catholic historians made no secret of the fact, and their opponents had no right to be scandalized at it. Soloviev expressed his opinion on the subject quite frankly.

In 1881 he ventured for the first time to criticize the spiritual power in Russia, and to reproach the Holy Synod for its inactivity. Love, he says, is always active, and a Christian hierarchy, with no love of Christ, has no right to exist. The task assigned to the spiritual authority is to spread abroad the spirit of love; it ought to effect a more and more perfect realization of the first three petitions of the *Pater Noster*. Now the sole result of the Synod's administration has been to multiply sects, in which hatred of the official church is the sole bond of union. Does the actual process of enslavement imply that the Russian hierarchy has ceased to believe in the action of the Holy Ghost ? If so, we could understand why it no longer even attempted to win the world to Christ through charity.

Criticism such as this was very daring in Russia in 1880, but the Orthodox party judged it leniently, because the Roman hierarchy was much more severely condemned than that of the Holy Synod. Soloviev went on to say that, in the West, the Pope has taken the place of Christ, and Protestantism ignores Christ altogether   He added that, amidst the general enslavement of mind in the East, Orthodox Russia alone had respected liberty of conscience until the eighteenth century.

Several of these reservations disappeared in the three discourses delivered in 1881, 1882, 1883, in commemoration of Dostoïevsky's death. In each of them Soloviev discussed the great novelist's idea of the Church; and no subject could have been better suited to draw forth from the speaker his own personal opinions.

In the panegyric delivered in 1881 Soloviev still restricted himself to generalities; he showed that the author of *The House of the Dead* aimed at expanding and uniting the minds of men, and that, at least in his later years, he perceived how the

Church, and, of course, a Universal Church, ought to be the true school of greatness, and the one stronghold where souls meet together.

In the discourse delivered on February 1, 1882, Soloviev struck a new note. It is in Christ alone, he said, that all mankind can find the principle of unity and freedom. This idea dominated all Dostoïevsky's thought, and acquired such supremacy over his mind that thenceforth Christianity ceased to be to him a distant imagination. It became a living and active reality, influencing all loyal souls and men of good will. Dostoïevsky would not have conceived of it, said Soloviev, as a finished temple, a marvel of architecture perhaps, but without a soul, nor as a flame hidden within each conscience. He desired it to shed its rays outward, and to expand the piety of individuals so as to affect the whole world. " His aim was to point out to the Slavs the furrow that Providence invites them to dig, in the field where the One Father of the human race calls all nations to labour together."

In these two panegyrics Soloviev's comments upon Dostoïevsky's works and thoughts might be criticized, but it still seemed that no one had any right to complain, except the most intolerant of the Slavophile party. The third discourse had a wider range of subjects, and attracted as much attention as the lecture given by Dostoïevsky himself in 1880, on the occasion of the erection of Pouchkine's monument.

After alluding to the material development of Russia, accomplished by Alexander II., Soloviev

.boldly attacked " the scandalous separation of the
East from the West. This separation has no right
to exist, and has been, and is, a great sin. At the
moment when Byzantium perpetrated this offence,
God called Russia into existence that she might
make it good. At the present time Russia is mature
and is attaining to fully self-conscious thought.
The question presents itself to her: ' Shall Russia
carry on the historical wrong committed by the
Byzantine Empire ?' " There followed a twofold
apology for the Roman Church. From the historical
point of view Rome had offered magnificent resistance to every outbreak of anti-Christian feeling,
to heresies, Mahometanism, and the pagan developments of modern civilization. Practically she has
never abandoned, but perseveres in her glorious
attempt to sanctify the whole human race: " Rome
is truly Christian, for she is universal."

It is easy to imagine the consternation caused by
such words; and it was intensified, rather than
diminished, by the closing passage regarding the
mission of the Russian nation. According to
Dostoïevsky, Russia was called to effect a rapprochement between East and West, to unite them in
the harmony of divine truth and human liberty.
" Let us not reproach the West with its faults,
however real; we cannot put ourselves in the place
of others; but, when others do wrong, we can do
right." The publication of this discourse did not
lessen its effect; on the contrary, an appendix
emphasized the leading thought in it. K. N.
Leontiev, a writer of Slavophile tendencies, tried

to claim Dostoïevsky as the promoter of a vague kind of Neo-Christianity, but Soloviev vigorously rejected this imputation. Neo-Christianity is, he said, nothing but pure humanism, and Dostoïevsky would certainly have had nothing to do with it, for he used to say: " Christ is known only by the Church; love the Church above everything." God designed the Church to embrace all mankind, rendered divine by Christ; since, as St. Athanasius remarks, Christ became man to make man God. This faith is truly Christian, and in agreement with Orthodoxy and the tradition of the Fathers, and it leads to a reality that the New Testament describes in two phrases—" God all in all," " One flock and one Shepherd." The Church triumphant will complete this harmony of the world, which cannot be the outcome of any Neo-Christianity without Christ, but which will result from men's common faith in the personal divinity of the Nazarene crucified by Pontius Pilate.

The excitement produced by this panegyric, pronounced on February 19, 1883, had not died out, when it was revived and intensified by the publication, in the same year, of an important didactic work. *The Great Debate and Christian Polity* caused in Russia a sensation comparable to that which Newman's famous *Tract* 90 produced in England. One chapter in particular gave much offence, viz., that on *Papism and the Papacy*. It showed that much darkness still obscured the author's mind, but the light was evidently breaking through,

10

and his honesty of purpose led him to give expression to some singularly bold conclusions. In these pages, with wonderful vigour and conciseness, he analyzed the religious attitude of Russia in his own day under all its aspects.

The great Debate is the antagonism between East and West, that has lasted for centuries, and dates back almost to the beginning of Christianity. From the earliest times and for various reasons, many being utterly futile, a conflict of tendencies has separated the two halves of Europe. In the East man is more contemplative, and willingly gives way to indolence and passivity; being selfish and lazy, he is apt to excuse his indifference towards his neighbours by pleading his devotion to God alone. In the West, on the contrary, man thinks only of action, and would readily be satisfied with a purely human greatness. He would be contented with a deified man, or even with the deification of humanity in the abstract, or of strength and genius. His innate tendency is to make human life, with its progress and activity, the object of his cultus.

The principles of Christianity restrain these different tendencies from excess, and lay hold of and unite what is good in each by revealing to the world the Man-God, God made Man. The West is free, therefore, to adore activity, human indeed, but humble, submissive, and resigned to pain. These virtues commend themselves to the Eastern mind, but it has to grasp the fact that God is not indifferent to the destiny of man, but deigned to impose upon Himself a thankless task and a painful

death, in order to save those whom He calls His
brethren.

These habitual tendencies cause men to rebel
against the teaching of the Man-God, where it
displeases them. The spirit of the West raises its
pride, intolerance, and the skill of its ruling class
in opposition to Christ; the Roman Empire had recourse to persecution in order to withstand Christianity. The more subtle Eastern character, on
the other hand, opposes Christianity by its gnosis
and heresy. It sought to exalt God very far above
man, so that the Father alone should be God, and
Christ His creature—this is Arianism; or His
helper—this is the heresy of Nestorius; or His
instrument, devoid of liberty and free will—this
is the monothelite version of an error that was
always fundamentally the same. Later on, the
same view of the relation between God and man
inspired the frenzy of the Iconoclasts in Byzantium,
and was responsible for the triumph of Mahometanism, which developed the twofold principle of
individual fatalism and of social passivity in the
presence of a Deity solitary, inaccessible, and
inhuman.

Evidently the saints, ascetics, and great monks
of the East and West preserved the true spirit of
Christianity, and struggled against the still vigorous
spirit of paganism, striving to restore and unite all in
Christ. But national exclusivism came forward to
thwart them, and in the East this became a recognized principle; Constantinople, the second Rome,
and Moscow, the third Rome, had from remote

ages been evolving the race spirit that rends the
Eastern Church, whenever a new State is organized.
The individual egotism of the East developed into
national egotism, and Byzantium, always richer
in theologians than in true Christians, strove to
find justification for this pagan apathy, as if Christ,
because He loved His country, for that reason
sanctioned all the narrowness of Judaism.

In contrast with these evils in the East, Soloviev
discussed those of the West, where also natural
tendencies had tried to reassert themselves, after
the first triumph of Christianity. Pride, the need
of human applause, a desire to replace God by man,
and the intoxication of power, had gradually perverted the hierarchy, and the Popes determined to
restore the ancient Cæsarism for their own advantage.
In fact, according to Soloviev, they were preparing
terrible disasters for the Church, and, following
their example, the kings and nations of the West
desire a universal dominion, that shall have absolute
control over men's minds and bodies. The con-
stitutions of Protestant States with the motto
Cuius regio eius religio, the Cæsaropapism of
Henry VIII., Elizabeth, and their successors, the
forms of worship organized and enforced, under
pain of the guillotine, by the Jacobin party during
the French Revolution—all these were modelled
on the example set by the Papacy.

At this point begins the central chapter of the
book, *Papism and the Papacy*. Before beginning it,
Soloviev gave a short summary of the opinions
already expressed. He believed that the conflict

between the tendencies of the East and West respectively had been the true cause of the great schism of 1054, the dispute as to the insertion of the word *Filioque* in the Creed having served as a pretext for it. The fact was that the spirit of paganism had triumphed on both sides. Without reflecting that they were about to divide the mystical body of Christ, the Eastern nations desired to secure their ecclesiastical independence, in order that their religious exclusivism might add strength to their national exclusivism. The Western nations had attempted to set up a purely human dominion, a violent and material absolutism, that should establish on earth the Kingdom of God. Such was, in Soloviev's opinion, the real cause of the long-lasting schism: human passions had taken the place of God's will.

Sometimes arguments are put forward, which are apt to mislead narrow minds, as is the case nowadays with the Polish question. But the Polish, the Eastern, and even the Jewish questions all revert to this fundamental problem: how can we secure the collaboration of East and West, of all who love Christ, either here or there, in order to realize God's design on earth, in sight of heaven, and add to His Kingdom, the body of Christ ?

Soloviev answered boldly: " Let us ask, not Papism, but the Papacy for the solution. Papism that is arbitrary, absolute, and violent must inevitably rouse the indignation of mankind; but need we condemn the Papacy in the same breath ? Let us try to be impartial; we Russians always dread

Rome as a foreign and even hostile power. Can we not see clearly that in every Kulturkampf of the West, the enemies of Roman Catholicism are at the same time opposed to all positive religion ? We cannot then ally ourselves with them. If we fancy the Roman Church to be like Peter, cutting off Malchus's ear, her enemies in the West resemble Judas; if we assume that, like Peter on Thabor, a Catholic talks like a parrot, and knows not what he says, his enemies in the West speak like those who struck Christ, and bade Him say who had struck Him, or like those who cried: *Tolle, tolle !*"

In contrast to anti-Christian coalitions, Rome presents to the world the spectacle of ecclesiastical union, centralization of the hierarchical authority, and affirmation of supreme authority.

Three questions will serve to justify or condemn this threefold claim on the part of the Roman Church:

1. Is the unity of a central power essential to the Church of Christ ?

2. With what right is this power connected with the episcopal See of Rome ?

3. What use has Rome made of this power ?

The first question amounts, as Soloviev says, to asking whether the Church as such, in spite of her unchanging character, has any right and duty to play a part in the world's history, and to make her own history on earth—viz., the history of her conflict with evil. If this question is answered in the affirmative, it is impossible to deny the necessity of visible unity, with a disciplined, hierarchical organization. Yet people maintain that this is contrary to the spiritual nature of the Church, for the religion of the Spirit can dispense with authority, being, like God and Christ, absolute truth.

Soloviev pointed out that this was a fundamental mistake, since God, Christ, and the Church are not only truth, but also authority—*Via, veritas, et vita.* In the first place they are the *way*, and this is necessarily objective and independent of caprice, in short, it is authority. Along this way the multitudes ought to advance in the midst of foes within and without, warring against the Church. They need the guidance of visible leaders, who walk with them and never lose touch with them. Under these conditions the religious advancement of Christianity must inevitably bring about a progressive centralization, in order to maintain unaltered the influence and visibility of the shepherds of the flock. The special mission of the bishops must be discernible at the first glance, and their union with one another revealed in the supremacy of the patriarchs. As early as the second century Irenæus taught explicitly that Rome was the only possible centre of ecclesiastical organization. Hence Irenæus supplies the answer to the second question, why Rome is the hierarchical centre of the Church. He points out that Providence, directing the course of history, has shown plainly that there is either no centre of the Church, or that it is located in Rome.

But what is the extent of this authority ? And how can we decide whether it has been exercised

legitimately or not? On this subject Soloviev
seems uncertain. The first part of his answer is
correct: The authority conferred by orders and the
sacramental power are the same in the Pope and in
all the other bishops. The words of consecration
are no less efficacious when pronounced by an
ordinary priest than when uttered by the Pope.
His personal duty with regard to revealed truth
requires him to profess the same faith as every other
Catholic, priest or layman. He is not the source
of revelation, and has no more authority than a
layman to change or add to it. Thus far Soloviev
is in agreement with the teaching of the Popes, as
to the power that they received from Christ; but
the second part of his answer to this question is
very inaccurate. Without considering whether the
primitive revelation did not require to be defended
against its enemies, and brought back to light,
he begins at once to examine what constitutes the
authority of jurisdiction that the Pope possesses,
and he defines it thus: The right to control all the
worldly business of the Church, and to concentrate
all her forces, in order to promote God's work in
every age. Soloviev here makes a strange distinction
contrary to his usual method, and, ceasing to
regard the Pope's mission as divine, aims at subordinating the papal authority to the personal
value of the man. " The name Head of the Church
cannot," he says, " be given to all the Popes; only
those deserve it in whom Christian humanity has
recognized the Eternal Pontiff." To these worthy
representatives of Jesus Christ, Eastern Christians

give without hesitation the title of *Caput Ecclesiae,*
ascribed in the Russian liturgy to St. Leo the Pope
(February 18).

In fact, continues Soloviev, the Pope's primacy
requires of him service rather than government,
and the man on whom this office is conferred ought
to think not of his own power but of the common
welfare of the Church. Judicial formulæ convey
no title in the Church; Leo and Gregory relied on
the faith and on the Gospel, and these sufficed to
obtain for them the recognition and obedience of
Christendom. These Popes exercised the lawful
authority of the Papacy. Others desired to promote
Papism and to subject all spiritual life to their
personal power; and thus, by a curious revenge
on the part of Providence, they brought about the
Protestant revolt against Rome—Papism was the
cause of the decay of the Papacy. Ever since the
Reformation, says Soloviev, the Italian Popes have
kept the spiritual power in the hands of Italians,
being anxious for Italy to hold sway over the world
of souls. Here, again, Providence has chastised
human ambition, and the national exclusivism of
the Popes suggested the first idea of Italian nationalism. The Italian Popes first originated and encouraged the conception of a united Italy, such as
has just been organized in opposition to them.

If these warnings on the part of Providence do
not succeed in reminding men that the Catholicity
of the Church should triumph over all private
patriotism, other chastisements will be inflicted;
a heresy originating with the advocates of a united

Italy might remove abuses, but its consequences would be more disastrous to the Church, to the souls of men, and to the Papacy than Anglicanism or Gallicanism.

Such is a brief and impartial résumé of this famous Chapter VI. Many people in Russia considered it a daring apology for Rome and a public declaration of apostasy, but to a Western critic it seems to mark a stage butl not a stopping-place on Soloviev's path. Our interest centres, not in the conclusions at which he arrived, for they are still very vague, and were soon revised by the author himself, but in his frankness and in the honesty of his attempt to understand and reconcile minds and hearts. We shall notice only this point of view from the last chapter, the other ideas in which will be discussed elsewhere.

To pave the way for a reunion between the Eastern and Western Churches, Soloviev begged each member of both to consent to do two things—viz., to render his own union with Christ more sure and close, and to revere in his neighbour's soul the active life of the Holy Ghost. Development of grace cannot take place without an increase of charity, and supernatural charity in souls leads to mutual understanding, and so effects a union of spirit, based on no artificial compromise, but on the truth of Christ, who is indivisible.

The storm raised by *The Great Debate and Christian Politics* forced Soloviev to define precisely his position. The trial of Newman before the Court of Arches had had the same effect in former years. In the first place the press accused Soloviev of

Polonism, but he had no difficulty in refuting this calumny in an article on *The Entente with Rome and the Moscow Papers*. In it he argued that to propose a diplomatic understanding with Rome on the Polish question, and a religious understanding with her apart from this question, could not fairly be called Polonism. On the contrary, such a proposal distinguished clearly the political and the religious questions. If the only representatives of Catholicism in Russia continued to be the Poles, national rivalry would aggravate the religious cleavage, but a nuncio, who had nothing to do with Poland, could act independently in both matters.

About this time Dr. Reinkens, Bishop of the Old Catholics in Germany, was seeking support from the Eastern Churches, and his appeal had aroused some sympathy in Russia. Soloviev was sounded on the subject, and asked whether the proposed alliance might not prove the means of reconciling the anti-Roman prejudices of the Russians with his own universalist aspirations. His answer was most emphatic, and more trenchant than perhaps any other of his utterances, for he was a man of gentle disposition. He declared the position of the Old Catholics to be fatally inconsistent. " Though I deeply regret," he said, " the separation between East and West, I understand it perfectly, and understand also their separate organizations, as well as Protestant individualism. The Church of tradition, the Church of authority, the claim to freedom—these three ideas account for . the antagonism existing between the supporters of

each. But have the Old Catholics any excuse at
all for their isolation ?   If their appeal to tradition
were honest, they ought to join the Eastern Church;
if they wish to throw off ecclesiastical authority,
they should call themselves Protestants.   In any
case they should abandon the use of the name
Catholic, because they are not inspired by any idea
of a universal Church.   They are, in fact, separatists,
endowed in the country that planned, desired, and
favoured their schism.   They might as well call
themselves ' Bismarck's Church.'   Russia has no
need of intercourse with people so isolated, but, on
the other hand, she cannot refrain from coming into
touch with Rome."

This opposition to the Old Catholic movement
intensified the suspicion with which Soloviev was
regarded, and increased the number of his enemies.
Without defending himself directly, he attempted
to convince, and so to disarm, his adversaries, and
returned to the religious question from a higher
and more general point of view.   A pamphlet
entitled *Judaism and the Christian Question* marked
the new tendency of his thought.   His exergue,
taken from Isaias, sums up eloquently the forbidden
thesis: " In that day shall Israel be the third to
the Egyptian and the Assyrian: a blessing in the
midst of the land, which the Lord of hosts hath
blessed, saying: Blessed be My people of Egypt,
and the work of My hands to the Assyrian; but Israel
is My inheritance " (Isa. xix. 24, 25).   The first
few pages show how great an influence the Jews
possess now in consequence of their wealth.   " Chris-

tian society is practically governed by the Jewish element; hence it is right, especially in Russia, to study not ' Christianity and the Jewish question,' but ' Judaism and the Christian question.' "

Was this the introduction to an anti-Semitic pamphlet ? Nothing was more opposed to Soloviev's idea. He begins by reminding his readers that in a public lecture, delivered at the University of Petrograd, he spoke in defence of the downtrodden Jews, and adds: " Wherever Christianity has been sincere, war on the Jews has been condemned by the faithful, whose sense of compassion impelled them to aim at instructing this unprogressive people in the true faith. The Popes have tolerated and protected the Jews." If Judaism is ever to be merged in Christianity, the union will be effected neither by material violence nor by religious indifference, but by the display of the true principles of Christianity in a Church resplendent with virtues. This Church, capable of enlightening the Jews, ought to shed its brightest rays upon Russia and Poland, since it is in these Slav countries, where Greek Slavs and Latin Slavs meet, that the centre of the religious activity of the Jews is to be found.

What must the Jews think of the Orthodox Church ? She persecutes them for no sufficient reason, and persecutes, too, the other Christian Churches, thus setting a detestable example, for the greatest fault of the Jews, a fault worse even than deicide, has been their national and religious exclusiveness, that grew more intense after Christ's resurrection. Of course the cross was a scandal

to the Jews, but their self-love was particularly
hurt when the Apostles preached salvation to the
Gentiles, and called all nations to be brethren in
religion.   Christians at least ought not to display
to the Jews their own disobedience to the same
commandment of Christ.

The second chapter, as it appears in print, ends thus
abruptly, but in the Slav Library at Brussels there is
a copy with manuscript notes by Soloviev, and at
this point he wrote: " Here the ecclesiastical censor
cut out about ten pages." Soloviev had given "Christian universalism " too Catholic an interpretation,
and somewhat later the censor again intervened.

In discussing the hierarchy of the Church, Soloviev said: " Its close and profound unity is due to
its divine origin, and this unity is shown visibly
in the life of the Church by the Councils. . . ."
In the printed text of the original pamphlet this
passage is followed by two lines referring to the
ecclesiastical supremacy and the absolute independence of the Councils.   In the copy belonging
to the Slav Library, Soloviev struck out these
two lines and wrote in the margin : " The censorship
of the Church here suppressed a passage bearing
on the importance of the Papacy."*

* It is much to be regretted that the editors of Soloviev's
complete works have given so few annotations. Critical
remarks on the MSS. of Soloviev, on the censor's alterations,
and the writer's reflections and protests would have been
most interesting, and might have thrown much light on the
history of Soloviev and his line of thought, as well as on the
work of the censor. Perhaps the importance and truth
of such remarks have led to their prohibition.

Soloviev pointed out that what he had written on the subject of the Byzantine Emperors' hostility to the Pope was suppressed, and replaced by an apocryphal text. These corrections affected the third chapter, that bears the curious heading: *Russia, Poland, and Israel.* Christianity was grafted upon Judaism by God, who aims at organizing human society into a free theocracy; but the new feature in Christianity is, besides theunive rsality of the Church, the visible manifestation of theandrism. The Man-God has appeared on earth, and remains the one true high priest, the one true ruler, the one true saint. *Tu solus Sanctus, tu solus Dominus, tu solus Altissimus,* as the liturgy proclaims. He has three means whereby He continues to abide with men: the Christian priesthood, derived from Christ and handed on by the Apostles; the administrative or ruling element in Christian society; and the inspiration of the prophets and holiness of the saints. We recognize here ideas that have already been noticed, but now Soloviev studies more precisely the origin, nature, limitations, rights, and duties of authority.

The Eastern nations of antiquity used to deify their sovereigns, and bow down before their unlimited autocracy. Ancient Greece required her rulers to be philosophers, justiciaries, and shepherds of their people, but for purely human reasons. Rome wished her supreme magistrate, whatever title he bore, to secure the supremacy of the law. Christianity groups all these elements together in a higher synthesis.

A Christian emperor forms part of the religious
order of the world, being the chief minister of the
truth and will of God, the defender and protector
of truth on earth. He is the supreme administrator
of justice, but responsible to Christ, of whose kingly
power he is the representative. Being anointed
by God and reigning by God's mercy, he is independent of popular caprice. By equity, therefore,
his authority is limited from above, not from below;
though he is the father and prince of his people, he
is the son of the Church. Christ consecrates him,
not, indeed, directly, but through the supreme
pontiff. This anointing does not bestow upon
the consecrator any direct rights over the State,
but it indicates the imperial mission in a Christian
society, and requires the emperor to be a loyal son
of the Church, and faithful in carrying out the will
of God.

To this supreme Tsar is delegated only part of
the divine or theocratic power. If he wishes to
control religion or reject the admonitions of holy
men, his exclusivism brings him back to the pagan
conception of imperialism. This tendency to
Oriental despotism proved the ruin of the Byzantine
emperors, plunging them into heresy and schism,
and making them neglect the spiritual welfare of
their people. Although Christian rulers, they forgot
their duty to the world, and did not encourage
missions that might have won fresh nations to
Christ. Their sin brought its own punishment.
Byzantium, surrounded by non-Christian races,
finally yielded to their pressure, and the triumph

of Mahometanism was a just penalty inflicted upon Eastern Christianity, which had been false to its duty of spreading the faith among all mankind.

Soloviev then proceeds to a weighty criticism of the Protestant principle. Of the three means whereby Christ was to continue among men, the Reformers wished to retain only the doctrine of inspiration. Having rebelled against pontifical authority, and the centralization, with its universalist tendency, of the Holy Roman Empire, their individual freedom of speech was often inspired by narrow nationalism, and degenerated. A Protestant preacher might, in the days of Luther and Zwingli, claim to be a prophet, or, like Melanchthon, be no more than a grammarian or a rabbi. In our own day Strauss is thoroughly anti-Christian, and others inculcate philosophical nihilism, or else are the docile slaves of the war party or of the plutocracy. Like the priesthood, and like the sacred character of the imperial power, the very semblance of faith in divine inspiration has vanished from Protestantism.

Only three organized bodies have preserved any trace of the theocratic government, necessary for the salvation of the world; these are Israel, Russia, and Romanism, represented to the Slavs by Poland. Israel, though retarded by its exclusiveness, remains nevertheless capable of becoming a race of saints and apostles, with great powers of organization, as soon as the narrowness of Judaism is broken down by the spectacle of unity amongst all Christians.

Russia has maintained the religious conception of imperial authority, and Poland, in spite of defeat, clings to her ideal, and is more faithful to the universalist or Catholic voice of the mind than to the Slav voice of flesh and blood. At the very border of the East she upholds the memory of the great Western pontiff, and we may well suppose that her mission is to bring East and West together, to set the Eastern Church free and to strengthen it by uniting it to the supreme pontiff, and at the same time to restore in the West the Christian dignity of the civil power.

" Indeed the greatness of the Polish nation consists in their carrying to the heart of Slavism, and representing in the face of the East, the chief spiritual principle of the Western nations." They have their faults, no doubt, but, says Soloviev, " I am writing for Russians, and it is not my business to examine the Poles' conscience for them. These representatives of Christian universalism would be traitors to Catholicism if they sacrificed their religious mission to their national aspirations. Have they in the past yielded to this temptation to exclusiveness ? It is not for me to discuss this question here; it is enough for me to point out to the Russians that the Poles are the instrument, supplied by Providence, for uniting the East and the West. How do we know that they may not be able to render Christianity the incomparable service of paving the way to reunion between the Eastern and Western Churches, and of bringing the Pope and the Tsar into peaceful alliance ?"

In speaking of union, Soloviev certainly had no idea of sacrificing the greatness of the Russian Empire, nor its national independence, nor the authority of the Tsar, nor the dignity of the Slav liturgy, so often approved, blessed, and protected by the Popes. In his opinion union with Rome was primarily a duty, but at the same time he thought that it would benefit Russia, and ensure the real liberty of the Eastern Orthodox Church, and its religious independence. He considered that such a union would immensely increase the importance of the Slavs in general, and of the Russian Empire in particular, not only in Europe, but throughout the world. It would bestow fresh prestige upon the Orthodox and Catholic Tsar, and, far from subordinating Russia to Poland, it would remove the true cause of their long-standing enmity. The union of these two nations of kindred race would be sanctified, as soon as they both bowed together to receive the Pope's blessing and to reverence the Russian Tsar.

CHAPTER IX

SOLOVIEV'S DEVELOPMENT AS A THEOLOGIAN:
QUESTIONS PUT TO THE RUSSIAN HIERARCHY
—HIS RELATIONS WITH MGR. STROSSMAYER
—" THE HISTORY AND FUTURE OF THEO-
CRACY "

THE breach between official Orthodoxy and Soloviev grew wider and wider, until the situation
became too strained to last. The ecclesiastical
censorship, always severe, showed itself still more
rigorous. The manuscript of a sketch of *The
History and Future of Theocracy* was confiscated,
and the most violent attacks upon Soloviev were
sanctioned and encouraged. To these, however,
Soloviev paid but little attention, for he had no
idea of a rupture with the Orthodox Church, and
was determined not to swerve from absolute loyalty
to her. Although threats were uttered, his conscience forbade him to abandon on this account
his honest inquiries, and without any concealment
he continued his quest of the truth.

Archpriest Ivantzov-Platonov had attempted to
refute *The Great Debate and Christian Politics*,
and his arguments may be summed up under two
headings: (1) History bears witness to abuses in

the life and government of the Popes; and (2) the primitive teaching of the Church regarding the dignity of the Roman Pontiff has been tampered with by scholastic theologians.

Soloviev replied: Possibly abuses and changes are to be found in what I call Papism; but how does that affect the Papacy ? Do these things justify our theologians in correcting what the Greek Fathers wrote concerning the importance of the Papacy in the primitive Church ? The Seventh Council, which is the last recognized by our Church as œcumenical, went further than any other in exalting the primacy of the Pope. Since that time we profess not to have heard the voice of the universal Church. How, then, can we admit any depreciation of the Papacy ? People talk, it is true, of the heresy of Rome, and say that the Popes became schismatics, when they inserted the *Filioque* in the Nicene Creed, in spite of the prohibition of the Holy Canons; and that, by admitting this doctrine, they became heretics.

Soloviev's keen insight took him straight to the heart of the matter, and he addressed nine questions on dogma to the archpriest Ivantzov-Platonov, and through him to the whole hierarchy. This time the sound of his voice was heard beyond the frontiers of the Empire; the Russian hierarchy might keep silence, but answers came from Paris and Rome. The following account of these questions is borrowed almost entirely from the translation of them that appeared in the French press (*L'Univers* of June 27, 1887).

First Question. When the Canons of the Œcu-

menical Councils require the Nicene faith to be
kept intact, do they refer to the letter or the meaning
of the Nicene Creed ?

Second Question. Does the word *Filioque,* in-
serted into the primitive text of the Council of
Nicæa-Constantinople, necessarily involve heresy ?
If so, which Council has condemned this heresy ?

Third Question. This addition made its appearance in the Churches of the West in the sixth century
and was known in the East towards the middle of
the seventh century. If it contains a heresy, why
did not the last two Œcumenical Councils (the sixth
in 680 and the seventh in 787) condemn the heresy,
and anathematize those who accepted it, instead
of remaining in communion with them ?

Fourth Question. If it is impossible to say with
certainty that the addition of the word *Filioque*
constitutes a heresy, is not every Orthodox Christian
free in this respect to follow St. Maximus the
Confessor, who in his letter to Marinus, a priest,
justifies the addition, and gives it an Orthodox
meaning ?

Fifth Question. Besides the *Filioque,* what other
doctrines of the Roman Church are heretical, and
what Œcumenical Councils have condemned them ?

Sixth Question. Is it possible that the Church
of Rome should be pronounced guilty, not of
heresy, but of schism ? Now schism, as defined
by the Fathers, takes place when a portion of the
Church (both clergy and laymen) cuts itself off from
the lawful ecclesiastical authority on account of
some question of ritual or discipline. This being

so, we may ask from what lawful ecclesiastical authority the Roman Church cut herself off.

Seventh Question. If the Church of Rome is not guilty of heresy, and if she cannot be in a state of schism, because there is no superior authority from which she could have separated, must we not recognize this Church as an integral part of the one Catholic Church of Christ, and acknowledge the separation between the Churches to have no truly religious and ecclesiastical justification, being merely the work of human politicians ?

Eighth Question. If our separation from the Church of Rome is based on no genuine principle, ought not we, Orthodox Christians, to lay more stress upon divine than human things ? Is it not our duty to labour for the restoration of union between the Eastern and Western Churches, and thus to promote the welfare of the entire Church ?

Ninth Question. If the re-establishment of intercommunion between the East and West is for us a duty, have we any right to delay its accomplishment by pleading the sins and shortcomings of others ?

In his *Answer to Danilevski* (1885), Soloviev reduced these nine questions to three. " You reproach me," he writes, " with being too favourable to Catholicism. But I write in Russia, where the works of Catholics, and of those who do them justice, are generally suppressed. I write in Russia for the Russians, and therefore I ought to insist upon both our faults and our duties. For even though the faults of the West may be more serious than ours, yet it is our own that we are called upon to correct. No matter who is to blame for it, the fact remains that the separation of the East and West was and is a worse misfortune to the universal Church, than the origin and development of Islam, which is, perhaps, the chastisement for the separation. Therefore surely no Christian should fail to seek an expiation for it.

In asking my three questions I had no other object than to facilitate a peaceable settlement.

1. According to my Orthodox assailants, the supreme and final authority in the Church, is the Church herself, the Church that is bound to tell me herself what the Church believes, for instance, regarding the *Filioque*. I ask therefore how the Church by herself can ratify and sanction the Councils.

2. The representatives of Orthodoxy are not agreed on the subject of Catholics. Some treat them as heathen, and even rebaptize them, whilst others, among whom are our greatest theologians, refuse even to regard them as heretics. I ask, therefore, how am I to know what the Church herself teaches about Catholics and their Church.

3. As the various nationalities belonging to the Eastern Church are not agreed in their attitude towards the Bulgarian Church, I ask how am I to know the opinion of the Church herself concerning the Bulgarians.''

Finally, after appealing to the authority of Stoïanov, Vostokov, and the great metropolitan Philaretus—the learned Philaretus who defined

Catholicism as " a true Church, but not altogether true"—Soloviev concludes that Catholics ought to be criticized and judged charitably, " otherwise, how can they believe that the essence of our Church is charity ?" Charity was destined to lead Soloviev much further, and to remove his last doubts.

These two lists of questions aroused such a storm in Russia, that it attracted attention in other countries, and made Soloviev's name well known in the West. The questions were discussed in Rome by Cardinal Mazzella, in a lecture given at the opening of the Catholic Academy. The Russian translation of this oration was published by Herder in 1889. In Paris Abbé Tilloy brought out an octavo volume of four hundred pages, with the title *Les Eglises Orientales dissidentes et l'Eglise Romaine. Réponse aux neuf questions de M. Soloviev.*

Before these answers appeared in the West, Soloviev had already published his own reply to his questions, but, owing to the severity of the censorship, he did not write in Russian, nor did his books appear in Russia. His first statement contained in his *Letter to Mgr. J. G. Strossmayer, Bishop of Bosnia and Sirmium* was printed in French, at Agram, and only very few copies of it were issued. It was dated September 29, 1886, and proposed to this Slav Catholic Bishop some considerations regarding the reunion of the Churches. This pamphlet consisted of only fourteen pages, but it did more than repudiate the " absurd inventions inspired by Byzantine hatred," and more than express the author's formal acceptance of " the sublime truth of the Immaculate Conception."*

It declared that in Orthodox Russia the mass of the faithful shared " the Catholic faith, apart from some doctrinal definitions made in the West after the separation, especially on the subject of the true character and attributes of the supreme power in the Church. On these points the Orthodox faithful were ignorant." Soloviev went on to say: " As there never have been (and, according to our best theologians, never can be) any Œcumenical Councils in the East, since the separation of the Churches . . our schism exists for us only *de facto*, and by no means *de jure*. What reveals even more plainly the uncertain position of our Church with reference to Catholicism, is that some individuals declare publicly that they believe the ' new ' Catholic dogmas to be the legitimate development of Orthodox doctrine, and so they can remain in perfect com-

* In several places Soloviev points out that the opponents of this dogma fail completely to understand it. The Immaculate Conception is not the Virgin Birth; it does not assume any miraculous intervention in favour of our Lady's parents; Joïachim and Anna brought their child into the world in the ordinary way. But the child's soul, in virtue of the merits of Christ, foreseen by God, was preserved from the stain resting on all other descendants of Adam, by the outpouring of sanctifying grace. From its creation, the soul of this second Eve was free from spot, and pleasing to God, *gratia plena*. This is the whole meaning of the Immaculate Conception, and as Soloviev said, the dogma expresses the traditional belief of both East and West. The physiological considerations that led astray the scholars of the Middle Ages do not affect this truth.

munion with the Eastern Church. I can bear
witness to this fact from my own personal experience."

In these words Soloviev definitely professed his
intellectual adhesion to Catholic doctrine; he
accepted even the word *infallible*, but the feeling
that made him employ the periphrasis "on the
subject of the true character and attributes of the
supreme power in the Church," made him express
his homage to the authority of the Pope, St. Peter's
successor, in Latin: *Pastor et magister infallibilis
Ecclesiae universalis.*

This declaration was not made impetuously nor
through any desire to flatter a Catholic Bishop.
Even before the censorship forced him to write in
French, Soloviev had stated the conclusions, at
which he had arrived, in an intimate correspondence
with General Alexander Alexievitch Kireev. The
latter was an earnest and fearless advocate of an
anti-Roman alliance between the Old Catholics and
the Orthodox Eastern Church. As early as 1881
Soloviev had confided to him his first Catholic
aspirations, and wrote: "I refuse to set the motto
Ad Maiorem Russiae Gloriam in place of *Ad Maiorem
Dei Gloriam.*" Kireev thought that the visible
Church no longer existed, but had to be reconstituted
on fresh lines, on a Slavophile basis. Soloviev
replied: "May not the visible Church, whose
unity is indissoluble, exist simultaneously among
the Catholics and ourselves? The separation may
be only apparent; the underlying reality is the
permanent unity." In 1883, three years before

he wrote to Strossmayer, Soloviev had made a clear and precise statement of the results of his theological investigation; in writing to Kireev he said that he was convinced, from his study of history and patrology, that there was no dogmatic novelty and no heresy in *Infallibilitas, Immaculata Conceptio,* or *Filioque.* In the same letter he remarked that Protestantism has three great defects; it has no apostolic succession; it has tampered with the doctrine of the Incarnation, and no longer teaches the perfect theandrism of Christ, God and man; and it has lost the plenitude of the Sacraments, and consequently Protestants are outside the Church. " Catholics and members of the Orthodox Church, being loyal on these three points, continue on the contrary to share the life of the Church in common. Therefore my motto will always be: *Ceterum censeo instaurandam esse Ecclesiae unitatem."*

In 1884 he wrote again to Kireev: " The censor wishes to remove the word *infallibility* from my manuscript. The whole question is, however, to determine whether Catholicism is true or false, and whether Leo XIII. is one with Leo the Great or not."

Therefore it is plain that the letter to Strossmayer, printed in September, 1886, was the outcome of long, conscientious work. Soloviev hesitated for a considerable time before writing it. He felt no doubt as to the correctness of his opinions, but he was not sure whether his conscience required him to reveal them publicly, or whether such a revelation would be opportune.

The history of this mental struggle is worth

recording. For a long time Soloviev had admired Mgr. Strossmayer, though he did not know him personally. He saw in him a veteran of the Catholic episcopate, and an ardent champion of the Slavs. In order to draw them to Rome and obtain for them the benefits that Rome can confer, the bishop worked with an ardour that was occasionally excessive, but always loyal.

At the close of 1886 Soloviev resolved to put himself into communication with him, and wrote him a private letter, headed: " Moscow; the Feast of the Immaculate Conception of the Blessed Virgin, 1885." To one acquainted with the prejudices of the Orthodox party, this simple heading was equivalent to a profession of faith. The rest of the letter was written with great reserve. The writer begged the bishop to give him an interview in Croatia, either at Agram or at Djakovo. He indicated his reason for making this request by saying: " My heart rejoices at having such a guide as yourself."

At the, same time a very persistent rumour was current in some of the Moscow papers, that Soloviev was contributing attacks upon Russia to foreign periodicals.

In order to put an end to these insinuations, on November 28 (December 10), 1885, he wrote from Moscow a letter that appeared two days later in the *Novoïe Vremia* (No. 3,864), in which he says: " I have just finished the *first* article that I have ever written in a foreign language for readers outside Russia. It has appeared in the Croatian

journal *Katolicki List,* under the title: *Eglise Oriental
ou Eglise Orthodoxe ?*   In this article I have spoken
of Russia with patriotic affection." Nevertheless,
the imperial police, having found out that Soloviev
was thinking of going abroad, watched him closely,
regarding him as a "suspect," who ought not to
escape their vigilance. For six months all movement was impossible, and it was not until June 29,
1886, "the Feast of St. Peter and St. Paul," that
Soloviev was able to write a second letter to Mgr.
Strossmayer and say: "I have at last been able to
reach Austria, and am now free to see you."

The bishop kept Soloviev as his guest for a couple
of months, and their mutual understanding and
confidence surpassed all their expectations. The
French publication, that we have already discussed,
was the outcome of their conversations.

In September Soloviev's first visit to Djakovo
had ended, and on the 9/21 of this month he wrote
from Agram a letter full of affection and gratitude addressed to Bishop Strossmayer. With easy
familiarity he reproached the old man with taking
too little care of his health; assured him that he
dreamt of him every night and longed to meet that
"worthy follower of Krizanic" again at Djakovo
and even at Petrograd and Moscow. Finally, he
asked the bishop for his blessing "with devotion
and veneration." With this letter he sent "the
little memorial" which the two Christians had discussed at great length, being anxious to develop
Slavophilism into Catholicism. The memorial was
to be printed, but only a very few copies were to

be issued for private circulation. It was very carefully edited, and appeared in a pretty white binding. According to the notes made by Strossmayer's private secretary, Milko Tzeppelitch, there were only ten copies of it; three were sent to Rome, one to Leo XIII., another to Cardinal Rampolla, the Secretary of State, and a third to Mgr. (afterwards Cardinal) Vannutelli, Papal Nuncio at Vienna. Three other copies were placed at Strossmayer's disposal and four were sent to Soloviev. Of these last, he presented one to the Slav Library in Brussels. It will be reproduced in full, among Soloviev's French works.*

This pamphlet, marking a new and definite direction in Soloviev's line of thought, was unknown in Russia, where no notice was taken of his first visit to Strossmayer and his friend Canon Racki, President of the Croatian Academy. The censor even sanctioned the publication, in the *Novoïe Vremia*, of some verses, written by Soloviev, that appeared under the pseudonym of Prince Heliotrope.

Soloviev, though convinced intellectually, was still uncertain as to the practical obligations resting on him. At the beginning of August, 1886, he told his mother that he should perhaps receive Holy Communion on the Feast of the Assumption, in the Orthodox Church, served in Croatia by Serbian clergy.

* The pamphlet was reprinted by Radlov in his collection of Soloviev's letters, but he probably used a rough draft or an inaccurate copy. We have noticed some fifteen inaccuracies, occasionally of considerable importance, some affecting the phraseology and others the subject matter.

M. Charles Loiseau in the *Correspondant* of
April 25, 1905, recalls an anecdote that is characteristic of Soloviev's state of mind in 1886. " The
intercourse between these two men (Strossmayer and
Soloviev), neither of whom had any reason to envy
the learning and influence of the other, had something so noble, fraternal, and touching about it, that
those who witnessed it can never forget it. At
Djakovo Soloviev had one of those symbolical
adventures that occurred at intervals all through
his life. Being in the habit of walking about at
night, he was pacing the long paved corridor that
all who have been guests at Djakovo must know
well. At least a dozen rooms open upon it, and when
Soloviev had sufficiently thought out his metaphysical problem he was at a loss to know which
was his own room. He was one of those simple-
hearted men who confess and ask pardon for their
absent-mindedness, and do not boast of it. He
cautiously tried first one door, then another, but
the third was locked, and he felt that his tentative
method lacked discretion, so he determined to
continue to pace the corridor. Towards morning
he noticed that a door, which he had passed perhaps
a hundred times, was ajar, and certain signs convinced him that at last he had found the right
room. At breakfast the conversation turned on
his adventure, and when Strossmayer gently rallied
him about it, he replied in a deep, quiet voice :
' When we are in search of the truth, or uncertain
regarding which moral resolution we ought to form,
it often happens that we hesitate before a door,

that looks as if it were locked, but needs only to be pushed.' "

How many more times was the door to seem locked to Soloviev ? What answer could he give to the difficult case of conscience that was troubling him ? In the profound loyalty of his soul, he believed that Providence had imposed upon him the task of effecting, no matter at what cost to himself, a rapprochement between Russia and the Catholic Church. Henceforth the aim of his life was to show by his example that a Slav, without ceasing to be a Slav, could and should expand his heart and mind to embrace Catholicity in faith and endeavour, and prove at the same time that Roman Catholicism completes, crowns, and unifies all that is legitimate in the traditional Orthodoxy of the East.

He resolved to state his views in a large Russian work, a sort of discourse upon universal history, in which the course of religion in the past would display to his contemporaries the universalist or Catholic design, which Providence has laid before them with reference to the future. This work on *The History and Future of Theocracy* was to be in three volumes; history, philosophy, and revelation were to be shown to converge, more and more in the course of centuries, regarding the chief individual and collective duties of mankind. Let us examine briefly this ambitious design. God, the Father of the human race, desires it to be restored in Christ its Head; and this Head of the Church wishes all men to be united with Him through the Church.

His aim is to bring them all together into one flock
under one Shepherd; and to perfect them in a unity
resembling the divine unity of the Trinity. With
this divine unity in view, the spirit of Christ strives
to manifest even now the charity and harmony of
His members, in spite of the diversity of their
works.

This visible unity is recommended constantly
by St. Paul, who teaches at the same time that, if
it is to exist and increase, even in a local Church,
there must be a hierarchy, which, being instituted
by God and representing Him, subordinates our
free will to other wills, that communicate to us
God's commands. How, then, in a Church, that
has spread all over the world, can harmony exist
and be the incontestable mark of divine protection,
unless there is a bond of union visibly connecting
the religious efforts of believers in Jesus Christ ?
This bond of union, the sign and symbol of universal
charity, and consequently also of liberty, has never
existed, and can never exist, except in agreement
with the successor of St. Peter. Thus the divinization of the human race by a voluntary acceptance
of a Catholic theocracy has been, from the beginning
of the world, God's design. The history of the
resistance offered by man, and the new devices to
which God in His mercy has recourse, forms the
great drama being enacted in this world, the apotheosis of which will be in eternity. The great
acts in this drama have been—the choice of the
Israelites and their instruction by the prophets, the
Incarnation of the Word in the womb of an Immacu-

SOLOVIEV AS THEOLOGIAN   179

late Virgin, and the aid of the Holy Spirit bestowed upon the Church to render her really universal, by reuniting all mankind.

This aid of the Holy Ghost has a history, and a new phase of it is in course of preparation—viz., the visible union of all whose loyal faith in the Church of Christ binds them to the soul of that Church. By means of this visible union, the body of the Church will be revealed in all its beauty, strength, and vigorous growth, having as its supreme eternal Head none other than Jesus Christ, but with a hierarchy subject to the authority of each successive Pontiff who represents the unifying spiritual power of Christ.

A free theocracy would not, therefore, consist in the universal subordination of all nations to the material kingship of the popes. Jesus Christ alone would reign supreme over all the religious, social, and material activity of this world, and the human representatives of this Divine authority would hold it only with limitations of time and space. The popes exercise this authority in spiritual matters, and temporal rulers in the domain of economics and politics. Both, being mortal, will have to render a strict account of their actions, and the thought of their responsibility explains God's patience with His stewards, even when guilty and scandalous in their lives. Scandals have existed in the case of -popes and kings, and human passions and selfish ambition have more than once corrupted those who ought to be saints of God, and disinterested servants of His earthly kingdom. Their most serious offence is the attempt to grasp all the powers that belong to Jesus Christ alone. If an emperor wishes to govern the spiritual order, or a pope to manage the temporal affairs of all the nations on earth, both are wrong; and this fault is committed by all who reject the union between Church and State. These two powers, each being a specialist in its own domain, affect the same persons and the same social forces; they cannot ignore one another, but should, on the contrary, be of mutual assistance. Their ultimate aims are identical. Both are God's delegates, and it is their task to organize mankind and lead them to God, so that the divinization, that He designs, may be effected.

There must then be an understanding between Church and State, but it must be in accordance with the interests at stake. The spirit is higher than matter, and so purely spiritual and religious interests must take precedence of economic prosperity and material development. The popes are commissioned to enlighten and direct the conscience of princes, to recall them to their duties as men and responsible rulers, to rebuke their wrongdoing, if of a nature to give scandal, and even to pronounce a solemn anathema against them. Hence the pope indirectly controls civil rulers, but this is not an encroachment upon their supremacy in the State, but a necessary result of the pope's spiritual power. The exercise of this power requires supernatural faith and courage; we cannot help admiring these virtues in the great popes, and regretting their absence in others, who, being weaker, shrank from condemning, in Christ's name, men of guilty conscience.

The carrying out of this design afforded Soloviev abundant opportunities of studying the historical grievances, that the Russians cherish against the Papacy. Some of them are the results of mistakes or false statements, others are based on facts. But men's faults do not overthrow God's work; the flight of the Apostles in the Garden of Olives did not cause their apostolic mission to be withdrawn. The Catholic Church never teaches that the man who is pope is impeccable, she only knows that God will secure the accomplishment of his social mission, and the infallibility of the Universal Teacher is guaranteed by Providence. The ultimate aim of this special protection is the divinization of the human race, that is called by Christ to a life of grace and free unity in charity.

Soloviev completed only one volume of this great work on *The History and Future of Theocracy.* He tried in the first instance to publish it in Russia, even before his visit to Strossmayer, but the censor absolutely refused to sanction its being printed. A few extracts from it appeared in the *Moscow Academy Review*, and eighty-five pages of it were published between September 8 and November 21, 1885 (*La rupture dogmatique dans l'Eglise et ses relations avec la question de l'union des Eglises*). This was, however, an insignificant part of a volume containing more than three hundred pages in the complete edition of Soloviev's works. The extracts

conclude with a note, in which the editor of the
Review states that he differs from Soloviev on the
Filioque question.

Greatly against his will, Soloviev had to publish
this first volume of *The History and Future of
Theocracy* at Agram.   On May 20, 1887, he informed
Nicolas Nicolaïevitch Strakhov that he had seen
it through the press; it was badly printed, as was
natural, since the printers knew no Russian, and it
had given the author a great deal of trouble.   He
hoped that the influence of the book would be worth
all the trouble and expense that it had cost him.
Of his own accord he had suppressed those passages
which would have most offended the censor, and
amongst them was a long discussion of the primacy
of St. Peter.   He trusted that the book in this
modified form might be allowed to circulate in
Russia, but he was disappointed; the censor absolutely forbade the book to be brought into the
country, and this prohibition, which was not
removed until after Soloviev's death, caused him to
desist from his undertaking.

In a letter dated October 12, 1886, Strossmayer
informed Mgr. Vannutelli, the Papal Nuncio at
Vienna, that the work would soon be finished:
Opus trium voluminum de unitate Ecclesiæ ; and in
December, 1887, Soloviev told Strakhov that he
was engaged upon the second volume.   A few
months later he wrote that it was finished, and that
he intended to cross the frontier in order to supervise
the printing.   However, on November 12/24, 1888, he
wrote from Agram to say that he had been obliged to

abandon his design. " I see no general advantage,"
he remarked, "in publishing Russian books that
will undoubtedly be prohibited in Russia. I have
not the least hope that the censor will moderate
his severity towards me for a long time to come."

These confidential statements show that a great
deal of interest attaches to Soloviev's unpublished
manuscripts. Their publication would throw much
light on the history of his thought, but, as it is,
we can only trace a few stages in it, being guided
by the landmarks that he himself has fixed. Outward signs of this kind, designed for the guidance
of others, do not always reveal the full depths of
a man's personal convictions, and more information
can often be gathered from notes and rough sketches,
in which remarks occur that prudence would forbid
him to publish, but that would reveal to us the hidden
secrets of his soul.

Soloviev's first visit to Djakovo coincides with his
adoption of a definite direction in his thought and
life. We shall see that during his journey to Paris
he expressed his views more decidedly, wording
them, however, so discreetly as to escape the censor's
prohibition. His conclusions had been prepared
in Russia, were formed finally in Strossmayer's
company with all the sincerity of ardent faith and
charity, and were openly proclaimed in Paris; they
never changed again.

The faith of his last twelve years was the subject of
a French book that will always be considered the chief
work of this great thinker, champion, and apostle
of divine truth—viz., *La Russie et l'Eglise universelle.*

CHAPTER X

THE CONCLUSIONS OF SOLOVIEV THE THEO-
LOGIAN: "THE RUSSIAN IDEAL"—"LA
RUSSIE ET L'EGLISE UNIVERSELLE"

TOWARD the end of 1886, M. Anatole Leroy-Beaulieu,
wishing to obtain " authentic information regarding
Soloviev's religious system," wrote to Father
Pierling on the subject. The latter forwarded
the request to Mgr. Strossmayer, who wrote in
reply a letter dated January 23, 1887. It has
hitherto not been published, and we reproduce it
in full, without altering the spelling.

REVERAND PÈRE ET MON CHER FRÈRE EN I.X.,

Voilà la lettre ecrite a moi par notre excellent
Souvalof (Soloviev). Il publira successiment 3
volumes, a Agram, sur la reunion des églises. L'im.
pression du premier volume est presque terminé-
Il a l'intention d'en publier un abregé en francais.
C'est un home ascete et vraiment saint. Son idée
mère est qu'il n'y a pas un vrai schisme en Russie,
mais seulement un grand malentendue. A present
il demeure à Moscou. Je lui écrirai instantanement,
qu'il vous expose un peu plus au fond sa doctrine.
Je cônais un peu l'excellent ecrivain Leroie-Beaulieu.
Je leus ses articles dans la revue des deux mondes.

Saluez le de ma part. Il est ami des Slaves. Il a mille foi raison. Il faut que la raçe latine, à la tete la france s'unisse à la raçe slave, pour se defendre contre la raçe altière et egoiste, qui nous tous ménace de son joug. Adieu mon chére frère. Je me recômande a votre charité et a vos prières.

Votre frère en I.X.,

STROSSMAYER,

eveque.*

DIAKOVO, 23/1, 1887.

A few days later Father Pierling received a letter from Soloviev, who wrote on January 31, 1887. The following are the most important passages in it: " Bishop Strossmayer has forwarded me the

* *Translation.*—Reverend Father and dear Brother in Christ. Here is the letter written me by our good friend Soloviev. He intends to publish three successive volumes at Agram, regarding the reunion of the Churches. The printing of the first volume is almost finished. He means to publish an abridgment of it in French. He is a mortified and really holy man. The idea with which he starts is that there is no actual schism in Russia, but only a great deal of misunderstanding. Just now he is living in Moscow. I will write to him at once and ask him to expound his views to you rather more thoroughly. I have a slight acquaintance with that excellent writer Leroy-Beaulieu, and have read his articles in the *Revue des deux Mondes·* Give him my kind regards. He is a friend to the Slavs, and with good reason. The Latin races, with France at their head, must unite with the Slavs, to defend themselves against the overbearing and selfish race that threatens to subjugate us all. Farewell, dear brother. I commend myself to your charity and prayers. Your brother in Christ,

STROSSMAYER, Bishop.

DIAKOVO.

January 23, 1887.

letter in which you expressed to him M. Leroy-Beaulieu's wish. This request for authentic information concerning my ' religious system ' affords me my first opportunity of laying my ideas before a really enlightened public. I am very glad of it, the more so because the persistent persecution of the censorship makes it almost impossible for me to address a public that is, strictly speaking, Russian. The work that you and M. Leroy-Beaulieu wish me to undertake agrees perfectly with one of my own schemes.

" I will myself write in French, as well as I can, a short but complete statement of my ideas on religion and the Church. I consider these two points to be of supreme and fundamental importance in the matter of reunion. I shall probably add to this statement a philosophical justification of the three doctrines of the Catholic Church that form the chief doctrinal obstacle to union between her and the Eastern Church—viz., the procession of the Holy Ghost *et a Filio* (*sic*), the dogma of the Immaculate Conception of the Blessed Virgin, and lastly *infallibilitas Summi Pontificis ex cathedra* (*sic*). All this will, when printed, cover eight or ten pages, and will form an article that I shall be happy to write under the title of *Philosophy of the Universal Church.*

" M. Leroy-Beaulieu can make use of this article, either in manuscript or in print, when he brings out his third volume. I earnestly beg you to write to me on this subject."

The suggested title was altered, and the article

became a volume containing four hundred pages. M. Leroy-Beaulieu did far more than utilize it for his own great work, and it was at his house in Viroflay that Soloviev finally completed the task that he had undertaken.

This French work occupied him for more than two years; on January 30, 1887, he told Strakhov what M. Leroy-Beaulieu had done, and communicated to him as a great secret the plan of his article. On May 20 he still spoke, in a letter to the same correspondent, of a work on the *Philosophy of the Universal Church.* On December 6, in the same year, he relates a very characteristic incident that he had witnessed: " I told you, I think," he says, " that a picture representing Christ in the act of giving the keys to the Apostle Peter has been removed from our Russian exhibition of Raphael's works." He goes on in the same letter to mention the title now definitely chosen for his French work; it was *La Russie et l'Eglise Universelle.* " In this book I shall be able to express all my ideas freely and fully." Finally, on November 12/24, 1888, he wrote from Agram to inform his friend that the book was being printed in Paris. Meantime various events had occurred which we must notice briefly.

For some years Soloviev had been acquainted with Princess Elizabeth Volkonsky, a woman of rare virtue and deep piety.* She was born in 1838

* The details given concerning Princess Elizabeth Volkonsky are derived from an unpublished private document in the Slav Library. Quotations from it are printed within inverted commas.

and belonged to an aristocratic Orthodox family.
Her early years were passed in Rome, where she was
remarkable for her religious fervour, and when she
married Prince Michael Volkonsky, she hoped to
gather round her a family equally devoted to the
Orthodox Church.

" She always believed in the Universal Church,
considering it to be the Church of the East, but she
felt no hostility towards the Catholic Church, with
which she had been familiar in her childhood."
Gradually, however, an uneasiness on the subject
of religion disturbed her peace of mind. " Her
character was too virile and her will too conscientious
for her to be influenced by mere impressions . . .
study, historical research, and reading the Fathers
of the Church led her in course of time to see the
truth." She was fifteen years older than Soloviev,
and had been struck by his first essays.

" Her friendship with Soloviev dated from 1880;
she understood him as soon as he came before the
public; she was his support when his enemies assailed him, and she did her best to obtain for him
liberty of speech. She put in circulation dozens of
copies of his first volume on Theocracy, and collected
money towards the expense of bringing out the
second volume. Soloviev did not accept the
money, and insisted upon her returning each
contribution to the giver." This sacred friendship
was strengthened by an interchange of valuable
services. Soloviev lavished his learning and zeal
upon the task of enlightening her calm, straight-
forward mind, and his personal conviction, the read-

ing that he recommended, and the work that she carried on under his direction, led at last to a practical result.

" In 1886 she visited Rome and received the blessing of Leo XIII., who introduced her to others who were also devoted to the task of reunion, and thenceforth she lived for this end alone, although she did not yet become a Catholic, for she thought that she could do better work by remaining where she was, than would be possible were she to attract attention by her reception into the Catholic Church, and consequently she deferred the moment so ardently desired." Soloviev induced her to postpone her entrance into the Church. Before his visit to Mgr. Strossmayer, he passed through Vienna on June 29, 1886, and called upon Father Tondini and Princess Volkonsky. For the second time he achieved the success that he mentioned in a letter to the *Novoïe Vremia*, dated November 28 (December 10), 1885. " I think," he said, " that ' conversion ' or ' outward union ' is useless, and even harmful. I have deterred several people from it, for our Church ought to be recognized as professing a correct faith."

The princess yielded to his persuasion, and spent some months in propagating prayer for reunion among the country priests of the Orthodox Church, especially in Carniola. " Her ardent desire was to succeed in instituting Masses for reunion in the Orthodox Church." To facilitate this design, she interested herself in the unification of the calendars, and in all the pontifical decisions that allowed Slav

Catholics to use a liturgy in harmony with their traditions and temperament.

Nevertheless she did not lose sight of the fundamental problem, and continued to ask herself what her personal obligations were. She was accustomed to literary work, having compiled a genealogy of the Volkonsky family, which was regarded as a model by the Imperial Genealogical Society. Now she began to arrange the notes on the Church that she had made when reading the Fathers, and, as soon as her Russian manuscript was completed, further delay seemed to her no less wrong than doubt, and she was received into the Church in November, 1887.

Her conversion was a shock to Soloviev, but he did not reproach her. If his own conscience bade him follow another path, it did not, in his opinion, require him to judge others.

In 1888 Princess Volkonsky brought out her first theological work—*The Church.* Soloviev had given her much encouragement regarding its publication. In September, 1889, appeared a refutation of it by M. Bielaïev, professor at the Ecclesiastical Academy of Kazan, who had sent the proofs of his work to Pobedonostsev, that they might be submitted to experts for revision.

In October Princess Volkonsky began her reply, and worked at it for years. It was published after her death, in Russian, by Herder at Freiburg in Breisgau, and bears the title *The Ecclesiastical Tradition and Theological Literature of Russia.* The author's name is not given. As her books could not appear in Russia, she was forced to work secretly and often wrote at night after returning from a ball or after long journeys. Sometimes for weeks or even months she wrote nothing at all. It is easy to understand that great mental weariness was caused by work so frequently interrupted, and by the moral suffering of being compelled to keep silence about the truth, whilst she was treated by her enemies as a liar and forger. She died in February, 1897.

These extracts from a private document are enough to account for Soloviev's feelings during his journey to Paris in 1888. He went thither to superintend the printing of his French book *La Russie et l'Eglise Universelle.* When he consulted the princess with regard to it, she begged him to suppress all bitter attacks upon his country, and he complied, but nevertheless, in spite of her remonstrances, he brought out a sort of résumé of the book, in pamphlet form, containing the passages omitted from his larger work. They are excessively bitter and contain a reference to the celebrated paper on *The Russian Idea* that Soloviev read on May 25, 1888, at Paris, in the salon of Princess Sayn-Wittgenstein, *née* Bariatynski. There was a large audience, including the élite of the faubourg Saint-Germain, some members of the Academy and several priests and journalists. M. Eugène Tavernier says that about sixty people were present, most of them belonging to the society of the faubourg Saint - Germain, besides a few Russians, to whom Paris was a second home, some foreign religious and three or four persons connected with the press. Soloviev was introduced by Father Pierling, and spoke in French so pure that his eloquence and assurance astonished M. Tavernier, who says that the paper, though short, gave everyone an impression of power. Soloviev's thoughts, however, were so far beyond the horizon even of the élite among his hearers, that he felt himself misunderstood or only half understood by many. The Russian alliance had not yet brought French and Russians into sympathy.

Vladimir Guettée misrepresented the Russian opinion of this lecture, when he published immediately afterwards a very much biased reply to *The Russian Idea*. His pamphlet, *La Russie et son Eglise*, ends with a phrase intentionally insulting and very characteristic of the writer: " Soloviev is more papistical than Bellarmine, or the pope himself." The lecture on *The Russian Idea* contained nothing startling. No doubt Soloviev looked forward to the incorporation of his dearly loved Russia with the Catholic Church; no doubt he insisted upon the duty of religious universalism; but these statements were not new; he had repeated them in all his later works.

Whether the reader be interested chiefly in psychology or in religion, he will be more inclined to appreciate whatever marks progress towards a personal, definite solution of the ecclesiastical problem. From this point of view the French lecture contained nothing that a dutiful son of Russia could not say to his mother, nothing that did not betray his ambition for her. It only raised the question of Russia's *raison d'être* in universal history.

" One sees this vast empire take its place, more or less brilliantly, upon the world's stage, and accept Western civilization on many points of secondary importance, whilst obstinately rejecting it in more important matters, thus preserving an originality, which is no less striking because it is purely negative. When we see this great historical *fact*, we are impelled to ask: What *thought* does it hide from or reveal to us ? What is the *ideal* principle animating this mighty body ? What new *message* has this new nation to convey to mankind ? What part will it play in the history of the world ? For the answers to these questions, we must not go to public opinion at the present day, for then we might have to change our minds to-morrow, but we must seek them in the eternal truths of religion, since *the ideal of a nation is not what it thinks of itself in time, but what God thinks of it in eternity.*"

We shall quote at some length Soloviev's development of this theme, because the original text is generally unknown in Russia.

" In speaking of the real and essential unity of the human race, we ought to think of mankind as a great collective entity, or as a social organism of which the various nations are the living members. It is evident from this point of view that no nation can live in, for, and by itself, but that the life of each is a definite participation in the general life of humanity. The organic function that each

13

nation has to discharge in this universal life is its
true national ideal, determined from the beginning
by God's design.

" But if it is true that the human race is one great
organic whole, we must remember that it is not
a purely physical organism, but that the members
and elements of which it is composed—nations and
individuals—are moral beings. Now the essential
condition of a moral being in this:—the particular
function that it is required to discharge in the
universal life, the idea that determines its existence
in the mind of God, is never imposed as a material
necessity, but only as a moral obligation.

" The vocation or special ideal assigned by God
to each moral being, whether an individual or a
nation, and which is revealed to the conscience
of this being as his supreme duty, has in every case
a real power, and determines the existence of a
moral being, but it does this in two different ways.
It is the law of life, when the duty is discharged,
and the law of death, when it is neglected. No
moral being can ever withdraw from the divine
design, that is his *raison d'être*, but it rests with
himself to bear it in his heart and life, as a blessing
or as a curse."

In support of this statement Soloviev referred as
usual to the people of Israel.

" The nation called to give Christianity to the
world accomplished its task in spite of itself, and for
eighteen centuries the great majority of its members
have persisted in rejecting the divine ideal that was
carried in its heart and formed its true *raison d'être*.

It is, therefore, no longer permissible to assert that a nation's public opinion is always correct, and that no nation can ever fail to recognize or reject its true vocation."

The application of this theory to Russia was thrilling, beginning as it did with an outburst of poetical enthusiasm, and ending with filial sorrow.

" Truly I think of the rays, presaging a grand future, that lighted up our history at the outset; I recall, after the original foundation of material order, the no less remarkable introduction of Christianity, and the glorious figure of St. Vladimir, the ardent and fanatical servant of idols, who, perceiving the unsatisfying character of paganism, and feeling a need of true religion, reflected and deliberated for a long time before embracing it, but, when he had become a Christian, resolved to be one in earnest. Popular poetry calls our first Christian ruler ' the beautiful sun ' illuminating our early history. That sun was followed by centuries of darkness and gloom, and, after a long series of disasters, the Russian nation was forced back into the icy forests of the North-East, brutalized by slavery and the necessity of labouring on a barren soil, and almost cut off from communication with the centre of Christendom. Russia fell into a state of barbarism increased by a stupid and ignorant kind of national pride, and when the pious Muscovite, forgetful of St. Vladimir's real Christianity, devoted himself to absurd disputes on minute points of ritual, suddenly, out of all this chaos of barbarism and misery, arose the colossal figure of Peter the Great.

Being filled with an enlightened patriotism that was quick to perceive the true needs of the country, he cast aside the blind nationalism of Moscovy, and let nothing hinder him in his task of giving Russia the civilization that she despised. He did not, like a mighty protector, summon this foreign civilization, but went to seek it in its own home, in the guise of a humble servant and industrious apprentice. In spite of the grave defects in his private character, he continued to the end of his life to set a noble example of devotion to duty and of civic virtues. A definite national work, that has had such precursors, ought to be great and magnificent; a country that, in its barbarous state, was represented by St. Vladimir and Peter the Great, ought to aim very high. But the true greatness of Russia is a dead letter to our spurious patriots, who wish to impose upon the Russian nation a mission in history that they themselves have devised. . . . Was it worth while for Russia to have suffered and struggled during a thousand years, to have become Christian under St. Vladimir, and European under Peter the Great, occupying always a place apart between East and West, if it was only that thus she might become a means of realizing the ' great idea ' of Serbia and Bulgaria ?"

These were not the words of a desperate man, for Soloviev never despaired; he only condemned narrowness in the name of wider and higher aims.

" We must not, moreover, exaggerate the fears of pessimists. Russia has not yet abandoned her *raison d'être*, nor been false to the faith and love of her early youth. It is still within her power to renounce the selfish policy and national dulness that would necessarily render our historical mission a failure. The artificial product known as public opinion, made and sold by an opportunist press, has not yet stifled our national conscience, which will discover a truer expression of the real Russian ideal. We need not go far to seek it, for it is already present, revealed in the religious character of the people, foreshadowed and indicated by the most important events and the greatest personalities in our history. And, if that were not enough, we have still more weighty and trustworthy evidence— the revealed Word of God."

This revealed word, silent as it is regarding Russia and all nationalities later than the time of Christ, is eloquent on the universalist obligations of societies and individuals.

" To share in the life of the Universal Church, in the development of the entire Christian civilization, and to share in it according to one's own particular strength and ability, is the one true mission and aim of each nation. It is a self-evident and elementary truth that no individual organ can be thought of as isolated and set in opposition to other organs, but as united with all the other parts of the living body. From the Christian point of view, it is undeniable that this quite elementary truth is applicable to the human race, the body of Christ. Christ Himself recognized the existence and vocation of *all nations*, when He addressed the Apostles (Matt. xxviii. 19), but He did not speak to any one nation in particular, because, for Him, they existed only in their organic and moral union, as living members of one spiritual body. Thus Christianity admits the permanence of national life and the rights of nations, but condemns nationalism, which is, in a nation, what egotism is in an individual."

This general truth is as applicable to Russia as to other nations.

" The Russians are a Christian people, and consequently, to ascertain the true Russian idea, we must not ask what Russia will do by and for herself, but what she ought to do in the name of the Christian principle that she professes, and for the good of the universal Christianity to which she belongs. If she is to accomplish her mission, she must with heart and soul enter into the common life of the Christian world, and use all her national strength in effecting, together with other nations, that perfect and universal unity of the human race, the firm foundation of which is given us in the Church of Christ."

Soloviev was approaching the real heart of the matter—his views on the ecclesiastical organization of Russia.

" The spirit of national egotism is not easily overcome. It has found means of taking root in our midst, without openly denying the religious character innate in the Russian people. Not only does it admit that the Russians are Christians, but it proclaims emphatically that they are pre-eminently Christian, and that the Church is the true basis of our national life; but this assertion is only an excuse for the pretentious claim to possess the monopoly of faith and Christian life, and to have the Church solely with us. In this way, the Church, which is really the immovable rock of universal unity and solidarity, becomes to Russia the palladium of a narrow nationalism, and often even the passive instrument of a selfish and spiteful policy.

" Our religion, as manifested in the faith of the people and in our public worship, is perfectly orthodox. The Russian Church, inasmuch as she preserves the true faith, the apostolic succession, and valid sacraments, participates essentially in the universal Church founded by Christ. If, unhappily, this unity is only latent among us, and not a living reality, it is because for centuries the body of our Church has been fettered to a foul corpse, that poisons her as it decomposes.

" The official institution represented by our ecclesiastical government and school of theology maintains at all costs its exclusive and particular character, and certainly is not a living portion of the true Universal Church founded by Christ."

Soloviev had never previously so clearly distinguished the popular faith of the Russians and the organization that professes to control it. Gentle as he was, Soloviev abandoned the latter to the judgment of Ivan Aksakov, a decided anti-papist.

" If we are to believe its supporters, our Church is a large but faithless flock, and the police are the shepherds, who, with their whips, drive the lost sheep into the sheepfold. Does this agree with the true conception of Christ's Church ? If not, our Church has ceased to be Christ's Church; what is it, then? A State institution that may serve the interests of the State and promote morality. But we must not forget that the Church is a domain, where no alteration of the moral basis is admissible, where no infidelity to the vital principle can remain unpunished, and where, if one lies, the lie is uttered not to men, but to God. A Church unfaithful to Christ is the most barren and abnormal phenomenon on the face of the earth, doomed to failure by God's word. A Church forming part of a State, of a ' Kingdom of this world,' has been false to its mission, and must share the fate of all the kingdoms of this world. It has ceased to have in itself any *raison d'être*, and condemns itself to weakness and death.

" The Russian conscience is not free in Russia, and religious thought is stagnant, the abomination of desolation reigns in holy places; speech, the weapon of the mind, is put down by the material force of the State; and around the Church we see, not angels of God, guarding its portals, but gendarmes and police inspectors, upholding Orthodoxy, and directing our consciences."

In conclusion, Soloviev ends this scathing criticism with another quotation from Aksakov:

" The health-giving breath of the spirit of truth, the spirit of charity, the spirit of liberty and the spirit of life is lacking in the Russian Church."

He then suddenly reverts to his distinction between the faith of the people, and the bureaucracy of the official Church.

" An institution forsaken by the spirit of truth cannot be the true Church of God. We must not abandon the religion of our forefathers, nor the piety of the Orthodox people with their sacred traditions and objects of veneration. It is plain that the one sacrifice that we ought to make to truth is the pseudo-ecclesiastical institution, so well described by the Orthodox author whom I have quoted, the institution that is founded on servility and material interest, and that acts by means of fraud and violence."

The Christian spirit of the masses and the genuine Orthodoxy of their faith required and had a right to be set free from the oppressive supervision of an administration that claimed to be ecclesiastical in character, but was, in fact, opposed to the true Church of Christ.

" Whatever may be the intrinsic qualities of the Russian people, they cannot act in a normal way as long as the thought and conscience of the nation are paralyzed by violence and obscurantism. Our first duty, therefore, is to let in pure air and light, to remove the artificial barriers which keep the religious feeling of our race in isolation and inactivity, and to open up a straight path leading to full and living truth. But people fear the truth because it is Catholic—*i.e.*, universal, and they desire to have at all costs a religion apart, distinctively Russian, and a Church united with the Empire. They do not care for this Church in itself, but value it as the attribute and symbol of their exclusive nationalism."

Those who refuse to sacrifice their national egotism to universal truth cannot be, and ought not to assume the name of, Christians.

"Preparations are being made for celebrating solemnly the ninth centenary of the introduction of Christianity into Russia. I think, however, that the celebration will be premature. Some patriots talk as if St. Vladimir's baptism, efficacious as it was to the prince himself, had been to the nation only a baptism of water, and that we ought to be baptized a second time by the spirit of truth and the fire of charity. This second baptism is absolutely necessary, if not for Russia as a whole, at least for the section of society that speaks and acts at the present day. If it is to become Christian, it must renounce a new form of idolatry, less gross indeed, but not less absurd and far more harmful, than the idolatry practised by our pagan ancestors and cast aside by St. Vladimir. I mean that new idolatry, that mad epidemic of nationalism, that is urging nations to worship their own image, instead of the supreme and universal Godhead."

God, who governs the universe, willed to establish through His Son, Jesus Christ, a Church with no limitations of time and space, a universal Church, in which "the past and the future, the traditional and the ideal, are not mutually exclusive, but equally essential and indispensable."

"The principle of the past, or of paternity, is realized in the Church by the priesthood. A universal or Catholic Church must have a universal or international priesthood, centralized and unified in the person of one Father, common to all nations, the supreme Pontiff. It is plain that a national priesthood cannot, as such, represent the universal paternity embracing all nations alike. The reunion of the clergy of various nationalities into one œcumenical body cannot be effected except by means of an international centre, real and permanent, with power and right to resist all tendencies to particularism.

" The real unity of a family, if it is to be regular and lasting, requires a common father, or one who can take his place. If individuals and nations are to be bound together into one family, the paternal principle in religion must be realized on earth through an ecclesiastical monarchy, capable of gathering together all the national and individual elements, and of being always the living image and free instrument of God our Father."

Thus true patriotism and genuine Christianity ought to impel all Russians to promote the religious transformation of their country.

" Thanks to her historical conditions, Russia displays the most complete development, and the most vivid expression of an absolute national State, rejecting the unity of the Church and suppressing religious liberty. If we were a pagan nation, it would be quite possible for us to crystallize ourselves definitely into such a state. But the Russians are fundamentally Christian, and the excessive development of the anti-Christian principle of the absolute State is only the reverse of the true principle of the Kingship of Christ, which underlies the Christian state."

A change of front is still possible, and, being obligatory, it offers Russia a glorious future, provided that she will acquiesce in it.

" The Russian Empire, isolated in its absolutism, is a menace to Christendom, a probable source of endless strife and warfare. But the Russian Empire, willing to serve and protect the Universal Church and social organization, will bring peace and blessing to the nations."

This study of the Russian idea led up to a decisive formula, that is not only the end of Soloviev's pamphlet, but the summary of all his intellectual activity and life-work:

" The Russian ideal, the historical mission of Russia, requires us to acknowledge ourselves members of Christ's one universal family. . . . There is nothing exclusive about this idea, which is but a new aspect of the Christian idea itself, and if, in order to accomplish this national mission, we find it incumbent upon us to act with and for, rather than against, other nations, this is the great proof that this idea is correct. For truth is only a form of Good, and the Good is incapable of envy."*

* The pamphlet on the Russian ideal was sent to Rome by Mgr. Strossmayer. On July 23, 1888, Cardinal Rampolla wrote: " I have forwarded the little book to the Holy Father, ea addens quae de auctore opusculi et de conversione in praefatis litteris patefaciebas. Sensa haec Sanctitas sua, quae omnes populos ad Christi ovile reducere intense cupit, et probavit et laudibus prosecuta est, ac

The Russian Idea, published in 1888, was the forerunner of *Russia and the Universal Church,* which appeared in 1889. In the third book of this remarkable work, the social mysticism jars somewhat upon a Western theologian; the boldness of speech and the continual use of symbolical language are in harmony with the taste of the East rather than with our own. Some comparisons and analogies might be inoffensive in Russian, but difficult to express in French. Yet, in spite of the defects in the latter part of the book, it is as a whole, according to M. Tavernier, " admirable in the knowledge, logic, and eloquence " that it displays. It begins with a long introduction, in which the author sketches, in broad outline, the history of the chief errors threatening Christian thought and practice since the foundation of the Church. He details " the inner contradictions of this revolutionary individualism " from which the world is suffering; he regards them as being the logical result of the habits of those spurious Christians, who were unwilling to bring their public life into conformity with their speculative belief. " The human race believed that it was enough to profess faith in Christ's Divinity, without taking His teaching seriously. Certain texts from the Gospel were so arranged that one could derive whatever one wanted from them, whilst men conspired to keep silence regarding

---

Deum ferventer exorat, qui id munus omnipotenti sua gratia hoc miraculum patrare potest, ut communia desideria exaudiat." (Quoted by Dr. Svetozar Ritig from the diocesan archives of Agram.)

other texts that did not fit in with these arrangements. They were never tired of repeating the
commandment: ' Render to Cæsar the things that
are Cæsar's, and to God, the things that are God's,'
in order to sanction a system that gave Cæsar *all*
and God *nothing*. They were careful not to quote
the words: ' *All* power is given me in heaven *and
on earth.*' They looked upon Christ as a sacrificing
priest and as an atoning victim, but not as king. . . .
Thus history has witnessed, as we do now, the strange
phenomenon of a society professedly Christian and
yet really pagan, not only in its life, but in the *law*
governing its life."

According to the law of charity taught by Christ
for the divinization of men, the Kingdom of God was
to be established on earth through the agency of
the Universal Church. It was to realize the triple
union so often mentioned by Soloviev in his Russian
works; the *sacerdotal union* or hierarchical organization of the Church properly so-called, the *royal
union* or agreement on the part of the rulers to render
the State truly Christian, and the *prophetic union*
or joint action of the saints in order to imbue
Christian society with the true spirit of God.

Our Lord prayed that all His followers might be
one, *ut omnes unum sint.* Now " all are one in
the Church, through the unity of the hierarchy,
the faith and the sacraments." " The priesthood
is a *fait accompli,*" but the State, in which all are
equal before justice and the law, cannot accomplish
its mission except by submitting to the Church,
that supplies it with moral and religious sanction,

and a firm basis for its work. What the State will
be in its relations to Christianity is a problem of the
utmost importance to the historical destiny of
mankind.

A society that is essentially Christian—*i.e.*,
governed by the law of charity, will always remain
an ideal not realized on earth; but the attitude
adopted by States and rulers towards the Universal
Church, according as it hinders or advances sacerdotal activity, will do much to retard or promote
the gathering of all men into supernatural brother-
hood in Christ, and the formation of " the spiritual
communion of all who are regenerate, and have
become sons of the second Adam." This is the sole
bond of true and effectual solidarity between
nations and individuals.

In the pages that follow, Soloviev sketches in
broad outline, but with profound penetration,
the warfare that, ever since the time of Constantine,
has raged concerning this conception of the Christian
State; the alternations of success and defeat, due
to the incessant efforts of paganism to reassert itself,
in opposition to the teaching, the spirit and the
Church of Christ.

Instead of abandoning its underlying paganism,
the Byzantine Empire attempted to justify itself
by tampering with the purity of Christianity. The
emperors almost invariably favoured heresies of
every kind, and their compromises between truth
and error were a source of trouble from the fourth
to the ninth century.

" Intimate relations between Church and State

presuppose the supremacy of the former, since the divine is anterior and superior to the human. Heresy assailed the perfect unity of the divine and human natures in Christ, in order thus to sever the organic bond of union between Church and State, and to secure for the latter absolute independence." The imperialist and pagan tendency was towards separation; the Catholic and truly Christian tendency was, on the contrary, towards union. Soloviev emphasized this fact, and showed in vigorous language how the Aryan, Nestorian, Monophysite, and Iconoclastic heresies had all tended to separate Church and State. " Each error in turn was overcome by the opposition of the pope, and consequently the anti-Christian despots of the Byzantine Empire finally made a direct attack upon what is, in the Christian Church, the material realization of the divine, the fixed point, the centre of all exterior and visible action, the image and instrument of God's power—the apostolic See of Rome, the miraculous ikon of universal Christianity." " A decisive battle had to be fought between the pseudo-Christian Byzantine Empire and the orthodox Papacy, which was not only the infallible guardian of Christian truth, but also the first realization of this truth in the history of the human race."

After the period of " imperial heresies " came that of the evolution of " orthodox " Byzantinism, " a new phase of the anti-Christian spirit."

In this portion of history the decisive part was played by a third factor, which had not the courage of the great Eastern confessors of the Church

(Athanasius, Chrysostom, etc.), nor the perversity of the heresiarchs. " The great majority of the higher clergy of the Greek Church belonged to what may be called a semi-orthodox or orthodox anti-Catholic party. Being by conviction, habit, or tradition devoted to dogma, they had nothing to say on principle against the unity of the universal Church, provided that the centre of this unity should be in their midst; and since, as a matter of fact, the centre of unity existed elsewhere, they preferred to be Greeks rather than Christians. . . . As Christians, they could not on principle be Cæsaro-papists; but as Greek patriots they could profess their preference of Byzantine Cæsaropapism to the Roman Papacy." These anti-Catholic and anti-papal reactions occurred at first only after the down-fall of a fresh heresy. As soon as the first enthusiasm over the triumph of Catholic Orthodoxy cooled down, a large proportion of the Eastern hierarchy began to regret that this triumph was due to the Roman Pontiffs, and some change was felt to be necessary.

A solution of the problem was discovered at length by Photius, who saw that the Popes would have no excuse for interference in the East, if the emperors would but refrain from legislation on points of dogma. If the anti-Catholic Orthodox party were reassured on this matter, they would gladly put up with a purely pagan State, social and political. The compact was concluded on these terms. The emperors once for all embraced *Ortho-doxy* as an abstract dogma, and the Orthodox hierarchy blessed the paganism of public life *in*

14

sæcula sæculorum. . . . It is a significant fact, though often overlooked, that after 842 not a single Emperor of Constantinople was a heretic or a heresiarch. The object of this compact was to proclaim aloud the particularism of the East, its independence of the Pope, and its disregard of the universal Church.

Thus this so-called Byzantine Orthodoxy was really nothing but heresy in a new disguise. This contradiction between professed orthodoxy and practical heresy was the true cause of the downfall of the Byzantine Empire. " To one who has not studied the anti-Christian tendency of the later Empire, the ease and rapidity with which the Mahometan conquest was effected must seem most astonishing. Five years were enough to overcome three great patriarchates in the Eastern Church; there were no conversions to be made, but only an old veil to be torn away."

Providence transferred to France and Germany the mission of establishing a Christian State. " This transference was effected by the only Christian power with a right and duty to effect it—viz., by the power of St. Peter, who holds the keys of the Kingdom." Sincere efforts to accomplish this work were made by great Christians, such as Charlemagne and Otho, St. Henry, and St. Louis, but their successors, the Emperor Henry IV. and King Philip the Fair, were jealous of the Papacy. The political advantage of Papal influence even in temporal matters was felt under such pontiffs as Gregory VII., Innocent III., and Innocent IV.,

exceptional men, able to deal with the details of
a vast and complex policy, and subordinating always
the temporal to the spiritual and universal. Many
others, however, by their personal faults, dragged
religion down to the level of things material. Such
were the successes and failures of righteousness
in the Middle Ages.

Even so, the Papacy, not having among its
supporters any truly devoted State, failed to bring
Western society into a Christian and Catholic
organization. "Peace based on Christianity did
not exist, and a supernatural intervention alone
secured the national existence of France."*

Modern States have tried to dispense with and
yet do more than the Church, but, apart from
material progress, what have they achieved?
Secularized Europe, at the end of the nineteenth
century, was given over to universal militarism,
national hatred, social antagonism, class enmity,
and, in the case of individuals, a lowering of the
moral force. Soloviev's ardent patriotism was
roused to indignation by his survey of past failures,
and he wrote: "The profoundly religious and monarchical character of the Russian nation, some
significant facts in the past, the enormous size of
our Empire, the great latent power of the national
spirit contrasted with the barrenness and poverty
of its present condition, all these things seem to
suggest that Russia's destiny is to furnish the

* This remark, made by a Russian writer some years
before B. Joan of Arc was declared venerable, seems
worthy of notice.

universal Church with the political power that she must have, in order to save and regenerate Europe and the world."

It is incredible that the patriotism of one who desired such a mission for his country could ever be questioned. In his opinion the first step to be taken was "to establish a moral and intellectual bond of union between the religious consciousness of Russia and the truth of the universal Church."

In these words he defined the object of his book. It is essential to bear them in mind, if we are to understand the author's conduct, and not be astonished at the symbolical conceptions contained in the third book. Soloviev wrote, it is true, in French, but he wrote for Russians, and was well acquainted with their habitual trend of thought. Under the veil of allegory, he induced his readers to seek the light. One of these allegories, very simple and touching, occurs at the close of his long Introduction.

A church was to be erected, and the architect, before going away, traced out the general plan and laid the foundations. To his pupils he said: " I leave you the firm foundations that I have laid, and the general outline that I have drawn. That will be enough to guide you, if you are faithful to your duty. Moreover, I shall not forsake you, but shall be ever with you in thought and spirit."

Soon afterwards the workmen began to quarrel; some said that they might as well leave the foundations already laid, and build a church elsewhere, keeping the original design. In the heat of their

argument the men went so far as to assert (contrary
to their real opinion, frequently manifested) that
the architect never laid, nor even planned, any
foundations for the church. Others proposed to
put off the building until the master himself should
return. Many workmen, after vain attempts to
build in another place, gave up work altogether,
and the most zealous among them devoted their
life to thinking over the plan for an ideal church,
whilst the majority were contented with thinking
of it once a week. However, even amongst these
separatist labourers, there were some who remembered
the great architect's words: " These are the firm
foundations that I have laid, and my church is to be
built upon them." And one man said to the others:
" Let us acknowledge ourselves to be wrong, and let
us do justice and give honour to our comrades, and
join them in rearing the great building already
begun. We must all work together, if it is to be
completed on the proper foundations." This man's
speech seemed strange to most of his fellows, some
of whom called him Utopian, whilst others accused
him of pride and presumption. But the voice of
conscience told him clearly that his absent master
was with him in spirit and in truth.

Between this long passage and the book itself,
Soloviev inserted a solemn declaration or explicit
profession of faith, followed by a prayer that reveals
his patriotism and Christianity. He writes: " As
a member of the true and venerable Orthodox
Oriental or Greco-Russian Church, which speaks,

not through an anticanonical synod, nor through the agents of the secular power, but by the voice of her great Fathers and Doctors, I recognize as the supreme judge in matters of religion, him who was recognized as such by St. Irenæus, St. Dionysius the Great, St. Athanasius, St. John Chrysostom, St. Cyril, St. Flavian, Blessed Theodoret (*sic*), St. Maximus the Confessor, St. Theodore of Studium, St. Ignatius, etc., that is to say, I recognize the Apostle Peter, who lives still in his successors, and who did not hear in vain our Lord's words: ' Thou art Peter, and upon this rock I will build my Church. . . . Strengthen thy brethren. . . . Feed my sheep, feed my lambs.' "

Soloviev's care to appeal to the great Oriental tradition whilst proclaiming his obedience to the See of Peter is very remarkable, and still more remarkable is his prayer to St. Peter for the " hundred millions of Russian Christians . . . a multitude full of strength and ardent desires, but with no true knowledge of its destiny." The hour had come for them to make common cause, in order to advance the Kingdom of God in the future history of the world, and to promote theocracy—*i.e.*, Christianity in public life, and in politics. This programme includes liberty for the oppressed, protection for the weak, justice and peace. " Open then to the Russians, thou keybearer of Christ, and may the gate of history be to them and to the whole world the gate of the Kingdom of God."

After this introduction in the first book Soloviev discussed the religious state of Russia and Eastern

Christianity; in the second book the authority of the ecclesiastical monarchy founded by Jesus Christ; and in the third book he tried to formulate a social application of the Trinitarian principle.

As these three books will probably be reprinted with annotations, it is unnecessary to analyze them in detail. It will be enough to draw attention to the considerations that reveal Soloviev's personal conclusions, for in the present work our chief aim is to bring into prominence his deep underlying thoughts.

The first book, which abounds in shrewd remarks, avoids all appearance of being a serious indictment of ecclesiastical separatism. Nevertheless, Soloviev's arguments lose none of their force, in fact, they gain in weight through being brought forward in a very concrete and vivid manner. Soloviev insists on the distinction already noticed between the orthodoxy of the Russian nation (which deserves its name, since the people are Catholic in their faith and piety), and the pseudo-orthodoxy of official theologians, which is anti-Catholic. " This pseudo-orthodoxy of our theological schools has nothing in common with the faith of the universal Church, nor with the piety of the Russian nation, nor does it contain any positive element." For a thousand years this pseudo-orthodoxy has been reduced to appealing to an Œcumenical Council, which ought to be declared impossible, and it owes its existence to the goodwill and support of the temporal power. No positive definition of the Church exists or can exist in Russia; neither the official hierarchy, nor the Old Believers, nor the Slavophile party could justify their idea of a Church.

Non-Catholics always abandon one of the two elements, the divine and the human, that ought to make up the Church Militant of the Incarnate Word. They shrink from the inevitable contrasts that are brought into harmony by this first union— the contrast between unity and diversity, the contrast between hierarchical autĤority and voluntary adherence, the contrast between doctrinal infallibility and confession of incapacity to explain mysteries, the contrast between the fundamental sanctity of the Church and the faults of her individual members, the contrast between her spiritual vitality and her material poverty, and the contrast between her catholicity and the universal hostility towards her centre. In order to avoid these contrasts, non-Catholics abandon on each point one or other of the two elements on which Christ insists, and the consequence is, that the one which they desire to save breaks down at once. For instance, the adherents of the separated Eastern Church wish to ascribe to it a real and positive *unity*, yet the very name that they give it denotes two nationalities, for it is officially described as the Greco-Russian Church.

There is no unity either of faith or ritual; with regard to baptism, the first entrance into the Church, Constantinople teaches one thing and Petrograd another, and consequently a man who is an Orthodox Christian in Russia, is a heathen in the eyes of the Orthodox patriarch of Turkey. From one end of the Eastern Chruch to the other abound most serious differences of doctrine, that threaten to destroy intercommunion, and occasionally actually do so. Enforced silence alone prevents us from hearing of all these public ruptures.

One note, however, is common to all these autocephalous Churches: " Each possesses a clergy that aims at being national and nothing else, and that must, whether it likes it or not, acknowledge the absolute supremacy of the secular government. The sphere of national existence cannot in itself have more than one centre, and that is the ruler of the State."

" The episcopate of any particular Church cannot, in its dealings with the State, lay claim to the fulness of apostolic power except by really joining the nation to the universal or international Kingdom of Christ. A national Church, that is unwilling to submit to the absolutism of the State, and so to cease to be a Church at all, must necessarily have support outside the boundaries of the State and nation."

At the end of this first book Soloviev discusses the curious idea of establishing a religious centre, a quasi-Papacy, either at Constantinople or at Jerusalem; and he arrives at the justifiable conclusion: " In the first place we must acknowledge ourselves to be what we really are—an organic part of the great body of Christians, and we must proclaim our close connection with our brethren in the West, who possess the central organ that we lack. This moral act of justice and charity would in itself be a great step in advance, and is indispensable to all permanent progress in future."

In the second book of *La Russie et l'Eglise Universelle* Soloviev expounds the new and definite opinions that he has formed. Fourteen chapters are devoted to discussing, with references to Scripture and tradition, the nature and powers of the ecclesiastical monarchy founded by Jesus Christ. The various objections, both ancient and modern, whether materialist or Orthodox, are considered and answered.

In the first book the course of argument elicited definite statements such as the following: " The Papacy, as it now exists, is not an arbitrary usurpation of power, but a lawful development of the principles that were plainly active before the cleavage in the Church, and the Church has never raised any protest against them."

" Our Lord, after praying that all His followers might be one, as if this were the climax of His work, desired to give this work a firm and organic basis, and so He founded His visible Church, and gave her one chief ruler in the person of St. Peter, in order thus to safeguard her unity."

" If there is any delegation of power in the Gospel it is this. No temporal government received any promise or sanction from Christ. He founded nothing but the Church, and He founded it on the monarchical power of Peter: Thou art Peter, and upon this rock I will build my Church."

The contents of the second book may be summed up under three chief headings:

1. The Primacy of Peter as a Permanent Institution.

" The constitutive basis of the universal Church is this: one man, who, with God's assistance, is answerable for the whole world. The Church rests, not upon the unanimity of all believers—for this is impossible—nor upon the always doubtful agreement of a Council, but upon the real and living unity of the Prince of the Apostles. Consequently, each time that the question of truth is propounded to Christendom, it will be solved decisively neither by the consensus of mankind in general nor by the advice of a few. The arbitrary opinions of men give rise to nothing but heresies, and a hierarchy, that is decentralized and given over to the mercy of the secular power, will refrain from taking any action, or will do so only in councils, such as the robber-council of Ephesus. Only in her union with the rock on which she is founded can the Church hold true councils, and determine the truth by means of authentic formulæ."

2. The Unchanging Authority of Peter.

" Peter formulated the fundamental dogma of our religion not by means of collective deliberation, but with the direct help of God, as Jesus Christ Himself declared. His word regulates the faith of Christians by its own force, not through the agreement of others—*ex sese, non autem ex consensu Ecclesiæ.*"

3. Divine assistance renders this Authority Infallible.

" It is no false opinion or wavering faith, but a fixed and definite belief, that unites mankind with the truth of God, and forms the immovable foundation of the universal Church. This foundation is the faith of Peter, still living in his successors; a faith that is personal, in order that it may be made known to men, and also, by divine assistance, superhuman, in order that it may be infallible."

It would be easy to make more quotations from this second book. The soundest arguments are presented in very original form, and are as pleasing as they are forcible. We cannot, however, quote one hundred and twenty pages, and the reader can, if he likes, refer to the original text. This reserve on our part will prove to Orthodox readers that we really desire to avoid all polemics, and to refrain from any remark that might hurt them. It is our aim to give a perfectly objective account of Soloviev's line of thought, and on this topic it seems better to refer to his own statements as they stand in the book; a choice of extracts might seem to have been made in a biased and unfair manner.

We have already referred to the somewhat strange character of the third book. Its very title, *The Trinitarian Principle and its Social Application*, might well cause surprise, although perhaps this surprise would have disappeared had Soloviev taken pains to express himself more fully. Cir-

cumstances forced him to send in his manuscript
before it was revised, or even quite finished. The
extraordinary title becomes intelligible on reference
to a passage in the second book: " The one cornerstone of the Church is Jesus, but, if we believe
Jesus, the chief rock on which His Church is founded
is the Prince of the Apostles, and, if we believe
Peter, every true Christian is a living stone of
the Church " (1 Peter ii. 4, 5.) These three truths
are apparently contradictory, but are really in
perfect harmony. Jesus Christ, the one cornerstone
of the Kingdom of God in the purely religious or
mystical order, appoints St. Peter with his permanent
power as the foundation-stone of the Church in the
social order, for Christians in general, and each
member of the Christian community, being united
to Christ and abiding in the order that He established, becomes an individual constitutive element,
a living stone of the Church. In this way, following
St. Augustine's method, Soloviev tried to discover
traces of the Trinity in the natural, material and
social order, as well as in Christ's supernatural
work, His Church and His sacraments. The appli-
cations of this principle are sometimes obscure and
sometimes arbitrary, as are those of the great
Bishop of Hippo, and they often need to be eluci-
dated by means of other passages in Soloviev's
works. His true ideas thus become intelligible,
and will be seen to be quite free from error.

Whilst he was engaged upon *La Russie et l'Eglise
Universelle*, Soloviev was planning other works.

From 1888 onwards he contributed articles to the *Univers*, a French periodical. On August 4, 11, and 19, 1888, there appeared in it a series of articles on St. Vladimir and the Christian State, written on the occasion of the nine hundredth anniversary of the conversion of Russia. On September 22, 1888, he wrote protesting eloquently against a letter from Cracow, that had appeared four days previously under the heading: *Coup d'œil sur l'Histoire Religieuse de la Russie à propos des Articles de M. Soloviev.*

These long articles seem to have escaped the notice of Soloviev's Russian biographers, but they well deserve attention. In contrast to the " bureaucratic " celebration of St. Vladimir's baptism in 988, they strike the note of Christian praise. A few passages may be quoted from them:—

" Just at the time when the refined Greeks were rejecting the pearl of God's Kingdom, it was picked up by Russia, that was still half barbarous. The pearl was covered with Byzantine dust, which is piously preserved, even to the present day, by Russian theologians, by bishops who serve the State, and by the bureaucratic laymen who govern the Church; but the pearl itself is hidden in the hearts of the Russian people." (Here, again, we have the distinction of which Soloviev was so fond.) " But St. Vladimir, before hiding it there, showed it to his contemporaries in all its purity and beauty, as a pledge and foreshadowing of our destiny." When he was converted, " he did not become a Byzantine or half Christian. . . . He accepted Christianity as a whole, and was filled with the moral and social spirit of the Gospel." " If the germ of social and political Christianity was planted in Russia nine hundred years ago, why did it not take root ?" " Because after the time of St. Vladimir, the Eastern Church resigned her powers to the secular government," which " was justified in maintaining its independence of, and asserting its supremacy over, a spiritual power that represented nothing but a particular or national Church, cut off from the rest of Christendom. When it is said that the State ought to be subordinate to the Church, we must mean the one, indivisible, universal Church founded by Christ. The head of the State is the true representative of the nation as such, and a hierarchy, that insists upon being national and nothing else, must, whether it likes it or not, acknowledge the secular ruler as its absolute sovereign. . . . The Church in her very nature is not a national institution and cannot become one without losing her true *raison d'être.* . . . The interests of Christianity are not directly committed to the national State; in order to uphold them, the State must subordinate itself to the international institution that is truly representative of Christian unity—viz., the Catholic Church."

" The head of a Christian State should be a son of the Church, and, if he is to be so effectively, the Church must possess a power independent of and superior to that of the State. With the best will in the world, no secular monarch can be the son of a Church of whom he is the head, and whom he governs through his agents." The authority of a prince and the lawful independence of his subjects, national greatness and international alliances for promoting human progress, can derive nothing but benefit to themselves from a religious influence affecting both high and low alike, and appealing to the conscience of individuals and of nations.

To the same period belongs Soloviev's plan for publishing in Paris a " review wholly devoted to furthering Slav interests, and especially to the reconciliation of the two Churches. This was a magnificent scheme, worthy of great minds, and altogether in keeping with the nature and immortal destiny of Catholicism."*

Nothing came of the design, for the Review would probably have been prohibited in Russia, and Soloviev preferred to work there, and with great courage, to which we shall refer again later, he returned to Moscow. Thenceforth he took pains to temper the audacity of his utterances, so that the censor had not much excuse for suppressing his books. For instance, in 1893 he did not venture to write two of the articles that Constantin Constantinovitch Arseniev asked him to contribute to the *Grand Dictionnaire Encyclopédique.* In his letter of refusal, he says: " With regard to Gregory Nazianzen, I should have to discuss his views on the development

* These words occur in a letter written to Father Pierling by Mgr. Strossmayer on August 29, 1887. The Bishop continues: " I shall of course subscribe to this review and zealously support this laudable undertaking in our country. . . . I beg you, dear friend and brother, to communicate this fact to the worthy man who is selected to edit the review."

of dogma, his opinion that it was necessary to keep silence regarding the divinity of the Holy Ghost, until the public conscience was prepared to accept this truth, and lastly his ideas on the episcopal councils, especially the second, that he considers the greatest scourge of Christendom. As to Gregory of Nyssa, I could not conceal the fact that, according to his teaching, the Holy Ghost proceeds also from the Son. All this would arouse the censor's opposition and would give P——v (probably Pobedonost-sev) the desired excuse for excluding me from work on the dictionary, in the same way as I am already excluded from learned societies."

Soloviev's reserve in his latter works does not indicate any change in his convictions; he only modified his tactics. Thenceforth his immediate object was to restore the true and elementary principles of Christianity in the hearts of men. If faith in Jesus Christ, the Saviour of the world, were to recover its dominion, if love of His work were to influence the intellect, soul, and activity of every Russian, there could be no doubt of their ultimate religious progress. Unity of love, not a purely official agreement, would complete the Church according to the Catholic designs of Jesus Christ (see p. 212).

This confidence accounts for both the prudence and the boldness that Soloviev displayed in his later works. He was bold in demanding the full application of Christian principles in statements of dogma, in individual morality and in political and social legislation. He was prudent in no longer.

proclaiming openly anything about Catholicism,
except such truths as would pass the censor, and
in veiling the rest under allegories more or less
transparent. The censor did not, however, relax
his vigilance, and, although his scrutiny did not
disturb Soloviev's peace of mind, it awakened in
him occasionally a desire to adopt a bolder line of
action. He was criticized in 1890 for having, in a
paper on Japan, praised the Jesuits and their great
St. Francis Xavier, and this made him return to a
previous project. As early as 1887 he wrote to
Father Martinov, expressing his indignation as a
man, historian, and Christian, at the innumerable
absurd calumnies current in Russia against the
Jesuits. Samarine's book, containing all these
calumnies, had just appeared, but in spite of appearances, this was an unsatisfactory work, and Soloviev
felt bound in common honesty to refute these false
statements in the name of Russia. He was well
equipped to undertake this refutation; he had
profusely annotated Samarine's text with marginal
corrections, and he had read widely on the subject.

The priests whom he consulted advised him to
undertake in preference works of more universal
importance, less compromising to himself. They
assured him that they were not alarmed by calumny,
and reminded him that our Lord had called those
blessed, whom men should revile, and persecute,
and speak evil of, untruly, for His sake.

Although he adopted a tone that the censor
tolerated, Soloviev did not alter his views.

His last work, *The Three Conversations*, ends with thirty pages in which his undying wish for reunion between Rome and Russia is expressed most eloquently. Even in the time of Antichrist, the hopes and duties of Christians, honest though separated, would not change. If union had not then been effected, it would be realized at that time, even if God had to raise to life the last Pope, and had to give the stray sheep another John to lead them to Peter, before the end of the world.

The great parable, that won for Soloviev the reputation of a prophet, because in it he foretold clearly the approaching defeat of Russia by Japan, sums up the coming conflict between the two cities, and describes briefly what would probably have been elaborated in *The Future of Theocracy*— viz., an attempt to predict the last days of history. The pagan principle, incarnate in Antichrist and his anti-Pope, seems likely to prevail over all Christendom; by a false semblance of goodness, it will seduce vast multitudes of persons, who aim only at their own advantage, and reveal the unbelief prevalent everywhere. No apostate loves God; his self-love leads him to despise our crucified Saviour, Jesus Christ, the Incarnate Word, the Son of God.

All who have foresworn Christ will gather round their deified Emperor, and their council, held in the Imperial Temple, will celebrate the union of all the various sects. This will be the apotheosis of the human, as opposed to the divine, and the orchestra will play the *March of United Humanity*.

Amidst this general treachery, the Pope, another Peter, will be true to Christ, and a little band of religious and laymen will stand round him, fearlessly chanting, even in the presence of Antichrist, the divine promise: *Non prævalebunt, non prævalebunt portæ inferi.*

Two other groups, very small in number, will also offer resistance: John, the Metropolitan, representing the Orthodox believers, and Pauli, the professor, in the name of some Protestants, will approach Peter, and together they will confess Christ, the Son of God, the Incarnate Word, who died and rose again for the salvation of the world.

The Œcumenical Council of hierarchical and lay Christianity will be infuriated against these three groups of faithful witnesses, but will be unable to prevent the Pope from uttering his *contradicitur,* and hurling his threefold anathema against Antichrist, who will, of course, determine to extirpate these fanatics. He will believe that he has succeeded in ridding himself of the Vicar of Christ, but divine intervention will prevent the death of the latter, and at this last moment, just before the cataclysm that is destined to overthrow Antichrist, the reunion of the Churches will be effected.

John, the Metropolitan, the representative of Orthodoxy, will cry: " My children, the time has come for our Lord's last prayer on behalf of His disciples to be fulfilled, *that they may be one ;* may our brother Peter therefore be able to feed these few remaining sheep of our Lord's flock." The representative of the last Protestant believers will also in his turn proclaim: *Tu es Petrus.* " Thus in solitude and darkness the union of the Churches will be effected. But suddenly a bright light will flash through the darkness, and a great sign will appear in heaven; a woman will be seen, clothed with the sun, and having at her feet the moon, and on her head a crown of twelve stars. ' Behold our Labarum, let us go to her,' will be the Pope's exclamation, and towards this Immaculate Virgin he will lead the two men, recently united with him, and all true Christians."

Thus the parable ends, and it was almost the last thing that Soloviev wrote. The dialogue in which it occurs closes with a remark showing that he had a curious presentiment of his approaching death: " The author of this history did not finish it. Being already ill, he said: ' I will write it as soon as I am better.' But he never recovered, and the end of his story is buried with him."

A few weeks later Soloviev died suddenly, whilst on a journey undertaken in order to visit his mother. He was only forty-seven, but his strength was already exhausted. We may wonder whether the friends present at his funeral ever read his great parable; whether they ever weighed the words with which the preface to *The Three Conversations* begins: " Is my present work my Apologia ?" Did they notice that in this last work, Soloviev complained openly of the censorship, although such complaints were of very rare occurrence with him ?

If they could answer these three points in the affirmative, they must know that Soloviev to the

last toiled to develop in Orthodox Russia a less
narrow devotion to the Church, and some day this
Christian spirit will lead to re-union. To the end
he prayed that men of goodwill, and especially his
Russian brethren, might at length agree in recognizing, as the true work of Christ, His universal
Church, founded on Peter, and entrusted to his
infallible rule.

Did all Soloviev's friends understand him? It
is not for us to say, but he himself thought not.*
One of his most devoted friends, Prince Serge
Troubetzkoï, at whose house he died, had to ask
for an explanation of *The Three Conversations ;*
and the notes that Soloviev wrote for ·him are
perhaps the last words that he addressed to the
public.†

Soloviev might have said, in the words of the
Ukraine poet, G. S. Skovorod, one of his intimate
friends: " The world has praised me, but it has
never understood me." Even those who knew

* In his panegyric of Soloviev, delivered on January 21,
1901, at the Academy of Science, A. Koni shows that he
appreciated his friend's aims, and says: " A desire for the
reunion of the Churches lived in Soloviev's soul to the end
of his days . . . and this desire lives on in the hearts of
many true believers."

† Golovine, who sympathized with Soloviev, stated in
1910 that towards the end of his life he possibly approxi-
mated to the liberal Protestants. As sole proof of this
statement, Golovine quotes a remark made by Soloviev
concerning Harnack's work on the dogmas of Christianity.
He asked: " Which stands nearer to God, the man who,
without believing in Him, keeps His commandments, or
the man whose faith is orthodox, but whose conduct

him best did not perceive the full riches of his
soul and his intense zeal; nor did they appreciate
the Christian ambition underlying his patriotism,
and the hopes for his country that formed part of
his faith.

Although he suffered from his friends' failure
to understand him, he accepted it with humility.
His perpetual self-sacrifice was due to the same
motives as his prudence with regard to the censor;
at the cost of his own suffering, he hoped to purchase
the right to proclaim to his friends and to the world
at large as much as they could bear of absolute
truth.

Therefore by preserving the influence that his
great qualities gave him, he was able to uplift
many souls and prepare them for further progress.
The grain of wheat, which in loneliness and obscurity
dies under the earth, produces, when winter is over,
a goodly harvest.

It now remains for us to examine more minutely
what this hidden treasure was, and when we study
Soloviev on the ascetical side of his character, we
shall understand his humility and goodness more
. fully.

---

reveals his contempt for God's law ?" This criticism
would apply to Catholics rather than members of the
Orthodox Church, and the parable of the two brothers, to
which it alludes, contains nothing in support of Protestant
dogma. Somewhat further on in his *Souvenirs*, Golovine
expresses his regret that Soloviev never admitted " the
fundamental legitimacy of the three apostolic religions."
This regret explains Golovine's previous remark.

CHAPTER XI

SOLOVIEV'S ASCETICISM

SOLOVIEV'S ascetical teaching, like the rest of his work, bears the impress of his genius, and, on the other hand, his lofty intellect enhances in a remarkable degree his austere asceticism. The conscientious loyalty that impelled him to direct all his actions towards what is good, is a testimony to his virtues, and renders intelligible his continual advance from one truth to another. His outward appearance betrayed his ardent zeal for goodness. In 1886, when he was thirty-three years of age, a woman took him for the famous Father John of Cronstadt, whom the Russians venerated as a perfect type of sanctity. Eight months later, on October 12, 1886, Mgr. Strossmayer, in writing to Cardinal Vannutelli, then Papal Nuncio at Vienna, said: *Soloviev anima candida, pia ac vere sancta est.* Viscount de Vogüé said that his soul lighted up his face, so that it resembled Christ, as depicted by Slav monks, Christ loving, contemplating, and suffering. Professor Sikorsky, who used to attend Soloviev's lectures, delights to recall the personal influence that he exerted over his students,

" his spiritualized body, and the purity of his face."

All who remember Soloviev, both Slavs and Western Europeans, single out his goodness as his most prominent characteristic. From the preceding chapters it will be clear that this goodness was free from cowardice and all tendency to compromise. Let us examine it on its positive side.

Soloviev was a philologist and a poet, a scholar and an artist, an historian, a philosopher and a theologian. He was capable of dealing with very various subjects in a masterly manner, bringing them into harmony, and arranging them in order, so as to be subordinate to his idea of the Kingdom of God in the world. His intellect, great as it was, did not surpass his goodness of heart. Of course his thoughts caused great excitement in Russia; they were those of a precursor, standing alone and exposed to attacks from two camps. The Liberals would have welcomed him as a champion of reform, and have valued highly his knowledge of Western affairs, if only he could have denied, eliminated, or at least concealed, his Christian convictions. He insisted that, without true religion, real progress was impossible, and therefore all human progress has its origin and *raison d'être*, its perpetual stimulus and its final end in and through Christianity—and this Christianity was promised, prepared, first revealed and then slowly realized, so that it is at once complete and progressive. Such views were unpardonable in the opinion of the Liberals, and the Slavophile party regarded them with equal disfavour.

Soloviev's fearless belief ought to have satisfied these official champions of the faith; but he refused to identify Church and country; he would not allow that the Slavs alone were predestined to salvation; he protested against every kind of exclusivism and denounced all that savoured of the idea: " No salvation apart from Slavism." This was enough to bring down anathemas upon him; the " genuine Russians," though still isolated, already existed, and they felt bound to abuse Soloviev.

His goodness, however, used to disarm his adversaries, and as a rule, whenever they came into contact with him, it forced them to esteem him and won their sympathy. He was not much over twenty when he began to lecture on philosophy, and his hearers, both in Petrograd and Moscow, without exception adopted his views on Positivism; Professor Wedensky says that there was not one left " unconverted." Professor Koni, in his discourse before the Academy of Science, states the facts with greater precision. When Soloviev's lectures on theandrism were announced at the University of Petrograd, there was an immense agitation among the students of all the faculties. " Who," they asked, " is this insolent fellow who dares to bring religion into the sanctuary of science, and darkness into the abode of light ?" A plot was set on foot, and there was to be such an uproar, that the first lecture would be the only one of the course. All the students were invited to attend, and when the appointed

day arrived, the faculties of Science, Arts and Law
assembled in full force.

The youthful professor had to face this huge,
noisy audience, which refused to give him the
ordinary welcome. All eyes were fixed on him,
but something in his expression even then inspired
respect, and although some ringleaders tried to
make a disturbance, very few followed them, for
the audience as a whole was fascinated by the
young lecturer, who began to speak of the Christian
ideal, of human greatness and of God's love for
man. His powerful voice, deep and well modulated,
rang out amidst a religious silence, as he did homage
to Christ, speaking of Him as the sole principle
capable of establishing the reign of true brotherly
love, and imploring his hearers to allow themselves to be rendered divine by Him. Suddenly
applause broke out, and it was unanimous. The
students of all the faculties joined in acclaiming
the man whom they had come to vilify, and thenceforth they thronged to his lectures, eager to give
voice to their admiration. It would be useless to
enlarge upon this incident; those who have any
experience of University life will be able to
appreciate it.

Influence such as this is far more than mere
intellectual prestige. Students are often unwilling,
especially in Russia, to relish any pious exhortations
on the part of a professor, and abstract arguments
alone would never make them accept an unexpected
and austere form of religious philosophy. The
hearts of Slavs, perhaps more than of other men,

demand something beyond intellectual reasoning, and we may be sure that the young professor, who converted Russian students of his own age, was no ordinary man, but one possessed of unusual powers of affection and devotion. His goodness and generosity made him sympathize with all in distress, and his efforts to relieve poverty often reduced him to extreme want. Tavernier writes (*Art. Cit.*, p. 16): " I have often seen him cross the street, at the risk of being run over (for he was very short-sighted), in order to give alms to beggars, whose presence he felt rather than saw. He used even to run after them to give them gold and silver coins. His friends scolded him without rousing his anger, but they did not succeed in curing him, and his unfailing kindness was notorious both in Petrograd and Moscow." His almsgiving was ruining him, but he would not abandon the custom, and he even begged money for the poor from his friends, and taxed his ingenuity to discover fresh resources. One year when food was particularly costly, he thought that a dinner every day was perhaps a mere matter of habit, and that if he himself dined only every other day, he could enable some poor man to do the same.

His generosity was so lavish that " he used to give away the money that he had earned by working day and night for two or three months. After an almost incredible amount of work he would be fresh and keen, and, whilst living on tea and vegetables, he was engaged simultaneously on the composition of several poetical works and of articles for reviews."

He felt pity for starving bodies, and still more for souls, that ought to be fed on truth and love of God—but who was to give them this food? This pity for the souls of men inspired all Soloviev's literary activity. He knew that all around him were hearts and minds hungering for the things of God, and no one seemed to understand their need. These minds, rebellious against dogma, and these hearts, submissive to no law, nevertheless receive innumerable graces from God, although they are unaware of them. Their perpetual dream and aspiration is to live and know, to possess and enjoy. Who will make them understand their own dream? Who will tell them: " Your inclinations and ambitions come from God and are the appeals that in His goodness He makes from afar. Far from being condemned by God, they express in an imperfect manner His designs upon you. Do you wish to raise yourselves above the level of humanity?* Christ came down to fill you with this desire to rise, to inflame your hearts, and to give you an example and the means of realizing your aspirations. Do you aim at being gods? There is nothing bad in this. It would be a sin to try to put man in God's place, or to drag God down to man's level, or to idolize yourselves, whilst you forget God or subordinate Him to your human nature. But if what you wish is to be lifted up to God, and united to Him, so that He may be in you, and you in Him; if you are

---

* Soloviev saw clearly the evil that Nietzsche's teaching was likely to cause in Russia, and alluded to it in several of his works.

tempted to despair, because, being eager to share
in the divine nature, you can but catch a glimpse
of it at an infinite distance, then take courage.
The Father, Son and Holy Ghost are calling you
to soar aloft to them; they are ready to come down
to you and take up their abode in your soul. In
return for your good will, they promise you an
incalculable reward, a mysterious transformation,
invisible at first, but afterwards radiant with glory;
and when you are united with and assimilated to
God, He will make you divine. Such is the faith
of Christianity and the revelation given to the world
by Christ, the Son of God."

Who was to say these things to the Slavs ?   They
were starving for the truth, and Soloviev, taking
to himself the words *Misereor super turbam,* for
the sake of souls entered upon his formidable
struggle with the philosophical and theological
errors current in Russia.

His learned and loyal explanations, and his
discussions, carried on invariably in a kindly spirit,
show that his object in view was to win over the
opponent, whose errors he was refuting, and to save
his soul. He wrote therefore without any bitterness,
party spirit, or narrow exclusivism. On the contrary he took pains, in dealing with any error, to
distinguish it from the truth that accredited it.
Then he proceeded to add to and elucidate this
truth, taking a comprehensive view of it, for he
knew well that the great enemy of truth is a partial
and one-sided opinion.

He avoided all personal polemics, although

occasionally he had to give a direct answer to
certain attacks. When this was necessary, he invariably displayed the greatest moderation, and
yet once he wished to accuse himself publicly of
having needlessly mentioned some of his critics
by name.

His extreme reserve was not due to cowardice
or fear of attacks; it proceeded from his respect for
the souls and intentions of men, and it was, moreover, his most successful stratagem. A statement
of truth, clear and convincing, but at the same
time most loyal and charitable, could not fail to be
a most effectual refutation of error. Soloviev's
tactics are most easily traced in his *Justification of
Good ;* this work, which is one of the most important,
is aimed throughout against the encroachments
of Tolstoïsm, and yet Tolstoï's name does not occur
once in the whole book.

No one could take offence at one who showed
such quiet calm in argument. He was in no danger
of being misunderstood and he displayed no trace
of jealousy or bitterness.* Soloviev's opponents
were forced to acknowledge that he respected them
and wished to do them good, and most of his readers
are fascinated by the peaceful spirit of his writings.
This spirit, being united with vigour of thought and
style, won for Soloviev respect and admiration, and
gained him many friends. Gradually the attacks
upon him ceased, and his enemies were put to silence,

---

* Tolstoï did not hesitate to commend his protégés to
Soloviev, who tried in every way to serve Tolstoï and had
hopes of making him see the light.

and towards the close of his life learned academies
and the salons of the highest aristocracy, political
assemblies and the embassies showered invitations
upon him.   He seemed to be on the way towards
enjoying the favour of the Imperial Court and the
applause of the populace, when death overtook him
unexpectedly at the house of his friend Prince
Troubetzkoï, at the age of forty-seven.

On his deathbed he murmured: " The service of
the Lord is hard," and his host, who caught these
words, adds: " The whole of Soloviev's life was an
attempt to justify his faith, and to facilitate the
action of the Good in which he believed.   He devoted himself wholly to his life-work, never pausing
to take breath, never sparing himself, but exhausting
himself by his zeal to fulfil what he regarded as his
mission.   His life was that of a combatant, who had
already overcome his own nature and lower inclinations.   This life was assuredly not easy; but
amidst his labours his spirit never flagged, because
he had kept his heart pure and his soul undaunted.
No sense of fear troubled him, and his courage was
the source of his gaiety and happiness, which are
the unmistakable sign and privilege of genuine
Christianity."   These words are an honour both to
the writer and to his friend, and they show us to
what heights Soloviev had attained by way of
suffering.   His sensitiveness was extreme and his
charity most delicate, so that his refined soul
suffered keenly from things that coarser natures
would hardly have felt.   Princess X. X., who,

both from her family traditions and as a convert, had unusual opportunities of knowing Soloviev, said that he needed affection and kindness. Instead of these, however, he received. for years nothing but abuse and calumny, and he often suffered acutely from attacks made upon him; in fact, it is possible that grief hastened his death, although he never displayed any anger or indignation. His soul was sanctified by suffering endured and offered up for the salvation of his beloved country.

Mgr. Strossmayer, who was intimately acquainted with Soloviev's aspirations and sorrows, bears witness to this sanctification. We have already quoted his letter to Cardinal Vannutelli, Papal Nuncio at Vienna, in which he speaks of Soloviev as *anima candida, pia ac vere sancta.* At the same time he announces that several important works were in course of preparation, and that a pilgrimage *ad limina* was in contemplation. He writes: " Soloviev et ego condiximus ut Romæ tempore sacerdotalis iubilæi summi et gloriosissimi Pontificis nostri conveniamus, ut pro consiliis et intentionibus nostris lumen et benedictionem efflagitemus."

When the Bishop carried out his design in 1888, he wrote to Cardinal Rampolla, commending to him "Vladimir Soloviev, a man as learned as he is pious," and worthy to receive from the Holy Father, at a private audience, a very special blessing upon his apostolate in Russia.

In another less formal correspondence, Mgr. Strossmayer spoke with less reserve, and what he says of his friend's sufferings will help us to appreciate more fully Soloviev's moral triumph, to which Prince Troubetzkoï's words already quoted bear witness. The old Bishop, writing to Father Pierling, on March 24, 1890, says: " We must support and encourage our friend Soloviev all the more because he has a natural tendency to melancholy, I might almost say, to despair. Let us love him, encourage him, and take him to our hearts. This is what I have done myself as far as my strength permits. I shall shortly write something in our papers on his work *La Russie et l'Eglise Universelle*, and I shall praise him as he deserves, to encourage him."

Again, on April 6, 1890, he writes: " Pardon my bluntness with regard to our good, pious Soloviev. He is, as you rightly remark, somewhat inclined to sadness and melancholy. Let us lift him up and encourage him, for he most thoroughly deserves it, but let us leave him his innate peculiarities. He seems to me to be a good instrument in the hands of Providence. Whilst we preach charity and peace, and the reunion of the two Churches, let us always remain in perfect charity and agreement. I am indeed delighted to find the same spirit in your estimable letters."

These occasional weaknesses in Soloviev's character did not cause Strossmayer to modify his first opinion: " Our good Soloviev is an ascetic and truly holy man." On Christmas Day, 1896, Soloviev, who was then at Tsarskoe Selo, and very ill, telegraphed to the Bishop, as he was accustomed to do on great festivals, to offer him his good wishes.

Strossmayer replied by telegram: "Thanks for congratulations. Your life and health are precious to the Church and the nation. Live therefore, we are all praying for you. I bless you with all my heart, and hope that your health will soon be completely restored."

Strossmayer was quite sincere, he attached the greatest importance to his friend's health and life. Being himself full of hope that better days were in store for Russians with Catholic aspirations, he desired Soloviev to witness this golden age. In the letter already quoted, that he addressed to Cardinal Vannutelli, he says: " In hisce horrendis calamitatibus . . . indubium est animas candidas et vere pias divino quodam impulsu *ad unitatem* tendere. Huius rei testimonium adnecto . . . quo evidens fit, in ipsa quoque ecclesia slavica orthodoxa pro unione promovenda et divinam victimam, æternum omnis caritatis, concordiæ et unitatis pretium, et pignus, cottidie offerri, et preces assiduas hoc sancto fine ad Deum optimum maximum fundi."

In his humility the venerable old man declared himself unworthy to see the day break, when so many Masses would obtain unity among Christians, but others seemed to him worthy to behold its splendour. He writes:

" Ego ipse ceu peccator vix mereor ut auroram adminus lætissimæ huiusmodi diei conspiciam; ast Soloviev et principissa Volkonski et aliæ animæ piæ et sanctæ merebuntùr certe, ut videant, si non lucem plenam, adminus stellam matutinam huius lætissimæ lucis, quam Pater æternus in consolationem eorum, qui in pessimis adiunctis non desperabant, sed vires suas ad unionem inpendebant, in sua tenet potestate."

The Bishop's hope was not fulfilled, and of the two friends the younger died first, before the " morning star " appeared on the horizon.

In his youth Soloviev had written some verses foretelling the loneliness of his religious life, and his words proved prophetic; they may be compared with Newman's " Lead, Kindly Light," written on his return journey from Sicily.

Soloviev's poem may be rendered thus: " In the dim morning light I advanced with timid step towards the enchanting, mysterious shores. The first flush of dawn was driving away the last lingering stars; my dreams still fluttered about me, and my soul, entangled among them, was praying— praying to unknown gods. In broad daylight I am walking, lonely as ever, through an unexplored country. The mist has vanished, and before me I behold clearly the steep path leading to the still distant mountain; how far off is all of which I have dreamt ! I shall go on till nightfall, walking fearlessly towards the desired country, where, high up on the mountain, in the light of new stars and sparkling flames of triumph, the temple stands resplendent, the temple promised to and awaiting me."

This promised temple is of course the glory of the universal Church. Soloviev longed to see it ever since he had shaken off the gloom that overshadowed his faith as a child, for thenceforth he never doubted God, or Divine Providence, or the work of redemption. He had sought new light regarding God's designs in the world; a mist hid them for a time, and, worn out by long-continued anguish of mind, he cried passionately: " My God, Christ Jesus, show me Thy work on earth, show me Thy Church . . . where is Thy Church ?"

At length the mist dispersed, and the temple promised to those who seek was revealed; it was the universal Church in the glory of her catholicity. From that day onward Soloviev was unwearied in pointing out to his brethren the City of God, set on a hill.   We have already quoted from the preface of his *Justification of Good*, in which he says: " The choice was always difficult between the various theories on the aim and object of life, and it is still more difficult in the present state of human knowledge.   Those fortunate persons who have already discovered for themselves a sure and definite solution of the problem are bound to convince others of its truth.   When the mind has triumphed over its own doubts, the heart cannot remain indifferent to the errors of others." These *others* for a long time seemed unable to see or hear what Soloviev meant.   Even the most sympathetic often failed to understand him, and at the same time the rigorous censorship forced him to exercise great prudence. After the solemn professions of faith that he had necessarily published abroad, his views had to be expressed with great discretion, if their publication were not to be altogether forbidden in Russia.

When Soloviev died, he had reason to fear that no one had followed him to the threshold of the

temple, but his works continued to point the way
thither, and thus light has already shone into the
minds, and love has warmed the hearts of many
people. Russians are now thinking over the Master's
solemn prayer: *ut omnes unum sint,* and comparing
universalism with Slavism; and as their faith grows,
so do their patriotic ambitions soar to greater
heights. Approach to the holy mountain is no
longer forbidden; even now some are brave enough
to attempt the ascent, and the eyes of multitudes
are fixed upon them. . . . Who knows what
Pusey might have undertaken, or Newman accomplished, in a Church with a valid hierarchy ? Who
then can foresee what the influence of the
Russian Newman may effect in the future among
his brethren ?

By way of illustration we may mention two
facts showing, no doubt, the difference of opinion
that prevails in Russia, and also the esteem in which
Soloviev is held. Early in April, 1906, there
appeared at Kiev the first number of a daily paper
called *Narod* (The People). The editor announced
that his programme was to spread abroad Soloviev's
ideas concerning universal Christianity. " Like
him, we desire religious society to be international,
and Christianity to control, not only private life,
but also the whole domain of social relations."
The method suggested was crude and questionable,
but the design was admirable : " To judge all subjects,
political and economic, philosophical and religious,
literary and artistic, from the Christian standpoint."
The editors of the paper, S. N. Boulgakov, pro-

fessor at the University, and A. S. Voljsky were
Orthodox; they declared that the newspaper,
though published in a provincial town, would not be
local in spirit: " We aim at interesting the whole of
Russia, and in gaining sympathy beyond the
frontiers of neighbouring nations for our publication
and Soloviev's ideas." The censor was on the alert,
and in spite of the feeling of liberty, that even then
was making itself perceptible, the paper was suppressed, when only five numbers had appeared.
The *Tserkovny Vestnik* (Ecclesiastical Messenger)
of April 20, 1906, did not hesitate to say that its
suppression was much to be regretted.

Just at the same time, by a strange coincidence,
the official Commission, that for six years had been
arranging for the convocation of a *Universal Council*
of all Russia, turned its attention to Soloviev.
M. Souvorov quoted his eminently Christian opinions
on the mystical body of Christ, and on the Church
as the City of God, described by St. Augustine.
These inquiries cast light upon Soloviev's dominant
idea: Our Lord, the Son of God, desired all Christians
to form *one* body, *multi unum corpus*, to be united
into one sole Church. ' On this rock,' He said,
' I will build *my* Church.' Christianity ought to be
known by this sign—its incessant effort to form a
Catholic temple.

Did Soloviev himself ever enter that temple ?
On the tenth anniversary of his death this question
was keenly discussed. We can only say what we
know on the subject.

He had long meditated upon St. Paul's words:

" I wished myself to be an anathema from Christ, for my brethren, who are my kinsmen according to the flesh." Soloviev, too, could say with perfect honesty: " I speak the truth in Christ; I lie not, my conscience bearing me witness in the Holy Ghost, that I have great sadness and continual sorrow in my heart " (Rom. ix. 1-3). One day Viscount de Vogüé overheard the following conversation: " But what about your own salvation ?" " What does my own salvation matter ? I must think of the common welfare of my brethren." *Optabam enim ego ipse anathema esse a Christo pro fratribus meis* (De Vogüé, *Sous l'Horizon*, p. 22).

Personal fear had no weight with Soloviev; in the course of the conversation to which allusion has just been made, he was warned that he would certainly be arrested and deported, if he returned to Russia from Paris. He was even told that orders had been issued to intern him in a monastery at Archangel. Vogüé writes: " We urged him to put off his departure, but he said: ' No, if I want my ideas to spread, must I not go and bear witness to them ?' " He was ever ready to bear witness to the truth at any cost.

The same opinion of Soloviev is expressed also by a Russian convert, a man of exalted rank, and full of courage, a high sense of honour and faith. Leontius Pavlovitch de Nicolaï was born in 1820 and died in 1891. Before his conversion he distinguished himself during the Caucasian War, when he commanded the Kabardinsky regiment against Schamyl. As aide-de-camp to Alexander II., he gained the Emperor's friendship, and then he sacrificed his whole career, was received into the Catholic Church, and became a priest and a Carthusian, in order to follow the truth and cross of Christ in a life of great austerity. On January 3, 1890, he wrote from the Grande Chartreuse as follows: " I well understand the reasons why Soloviev has practised a kind of reserve, which he imposed upon himself in the interest of the mission that he has to accomplish, and that has, no doubt, been assigned to him by the Most High. For the sake of his cause, he must cling to the Oriental rite, for if he adopted the Roman rite, he would cut the ground from under his feet in Russia, and all his work would be frustrated. . . . I used to hope that he would take some steps to render his attitude regular with reference to the Holy See, in order to put an end to every kind of doubt. I look upon the presentation of his book to the Holy Father by Mgr. Strossmayer as a first step in this direction. It was, I think, a profession of faith, frank and at the same time diplomatic, considering the delicacy of his position, and his obligation to have recourse to many expedients in order to avoid prejudice and persecution at home and from the whole bureaucratic tribe, with Pobedonostsev at its head. . . .

". . . He was well advised to go back to Russia, and not to listen to the voice of human prudence, that sought to dissuade him. His bold action must certainly have pleased the Emperor and all men of courage, and no doubt increased his prestige. . . .

" It would be a grand thing if he could definitely

raise the question of reunion between the Churches.
I have a firm conviction, which is shared by Soloviev,
that Russia would then be called to play a providential part either in the East or the West. . . .

"I maintain, and always shall maintain, that the
salvation and greatness of Russia depend entirely
upon the preservation of a religious spirit among
the masses (for the so-called higher classes are
already corrupt), and this spirit cannot be preserved
except by the Church, which must be such as Christ
desires, in union with the universal Church and her
supreme head. . . . Soloviev understands all this
perfectly, and is hovering aloft, soaring like an eagle.
I offer him true admiration and genuine sympathy.
. . . May God bless his work !"

These passages explain why no thought of *Latinization* ever entered Soloviev's mind; it would have
seemed to him a breach of faith towards his personal
mission, and an act of disobedience to the will of
the Popes, who from the earliest period down to the
present day have always upheld the lawful and
sacred character of the Oriental rites. They even
forbade any change of ritual to be proposed.
Soloviev intended to be a member of the universal
Roman Catholic Church, but not a *Latin* member,
for in his letter on the union of the Churches he
wrote: "It is the Church of Rome, not the Latin
Church, that is the *mater et magistra omnium
Ecclesiarum ;* it is the Bishop of Rome, and not the
Western patriarch, who speaks infallibly *ex cathedra*,
and we ought not to forget that there was a time
when the Bishops of Rome were Greeks."

On the other hand, the persecution organized by the Russian bureaucracy had destroyed all the branches in Russia, which, though not Latin, were in visible union with the great Roman trunk, and they were absolutely prevented from shooting out again. This intolerance made it impossible for Soloviev to bring his practice of religion into conformity with his profession of faith; and, accordingly, he urged again and again his entreaties that the State should guarantee liberty to use the Oriental rites, in the case of Christian communities not subject to the Holy Synod. This permission was partially granted by laws enacted in 1904 and 1905, but Soloviev had then been dead some years. If he ever took the decisive step of seeking admission to the Catholic Church, he must necessarily have done so secretly.

His friends knew nothing beyond the fact that this man, so full of faith, so irreproachable in his life, so good, pious, and austere, had ceased to receive the sacraments of the Orthodox Church. In 1892, during a serious illness, he received them for the last time from Father Orlov. He never approached them again, and secret instructions were given to the clergy to refuse communion to him as a " suspect."

Those who were aware of Soloviev's enthusiastic reverence and love for the Holy Eucharist, knew that there was some painful mystery on the subject, but were in the dark as to its nature. It was, however, revealed on the tenth anniversary of Soloviev's death, when the following facts were disclosed.

Nicolas Tolstoï, a priest ordained in the Established Church of Russia, but reconciled in 1893 to the Catholic Church, was continuing his ministry according to the ancient Slav rite of the East.* The fact that from time to time this priest was allowed to stay in Russia, removed the last obstacle in Soloviev's way, and " he who had long preached union with Rome among his fellow-countrymen now preached it also by his example, and made his complete submission to the Roman Church in the presence of several witnesses, in the Chapel of Our Lady of Lourdes at Moscow on February 18, 1896, being the second Sunday in Lent."†

Some Russian periodicals, such as the *Tserkov*, the *Rousskoïe Slovo* and the *Sovremennoïe Slovo*, published particulars rendering this statement more complete. There was no formal abjuration, for it was considered unnecessary. Soloviev solemnly read aloud his profession of faith, and added the declaration to which we have already referred: " As a member of the true and venerable Orthodox Oriental or Greco-Russian Church, which speaks not through an anticanonical synod, nor through the agents of the secular power . . . I recognize as the supreme judge in matters of religion . . . the apostle Peter, who lives still in his successors,

* On November 13, 1910, the Church of San Lorenzo di Monti in Rome, set apart for Catholics using this rite, was solemnly dedicated with pontifical Mass. The priest in charge, Father Verighine, is a Russian, very loyal to the ancient Slav liturgy.

† Article by Nicolas Tolstoï in the *Univers*, September 9, 1910,

and who did not hear in vain our Lord's words "
(*cf.* p. 213).

This formula, which Soloviev printed in 1889,
defines precisely what he meant by saying: " I
belong to the true Orthodox Church; it is in order
to profess our traditional Orthodoxy in all its
fulness, that, without being a Latin, I recognize
Rome as the centre of the whole of Christendom."

The witnesses of this approximation of " the
Russia of the future " to Rome were some members
of Father Tolstoï's family, his servants and a few
well-known inhabitants of Petrograd and Moscow.
On the following day Tolstoï was arrested, but the
authorities connived at his escape, and a few days
afterwards he was in Rome, having gone thither
to offer to the Holy Father the respectful homage
of his new spiritual son. At least Soloviev believed
this to be the reason of his journey, and thought
that Leo XIII. approved of what had taken place.

It is said that several of Soloviev's admirers,
under the influence of his works and example, were
not contented with expanding their own private
religion until it attained to catholicity of faith and
charity, but actually petitioned Rome to give them
Soloviev as their first Bishop. They were over-hasty
in their action. Leo XIII., who raised Newman to
the dignity of Cardinal, would, it is said, have sanctioned their choice, but he put off the execution of
this plan to a more favourable moment, and before
that moment arrived, Vladimir Serguievitch Soloviev
had died, being still a layman. He fell ill suddenly
whilst travelling, and as he was at Ouskoïe, in a

country house belonging to Prince Troubetzkoï, the only priest within reach was the Orthodox village priest, S. A. Bielaïev. In such a case every Catholic is entitled and almost bound to ask for absolution and the viaticum, and Soloviev, having done so, and being purified by this last gift of God, died and retracted nothing that he had taught.*

Extremists on both sides express very contradictory opinions regarding Soloviev's death, and both are equally mistaken. Those who talk of a return to the official Church have no ground for their joy, nor have those who charge this " Catholic Bishop " with hypocrisy any reason for their anger.

In February, 1911, a notice of Soloviev appeared in the *Messager Historique*, published at Petrograd. The writer, M. Gnédine, was acquainted with Vladimir Soloviev and his elder brother Vsevolod between 1870 and 1880. He used to read his works aloud to them, and the two brothers listened with enthusiastic admiration. He met them again in the publishing offices of the chief Russian periodicals, but subsequently lost sight of them. He tells us that one day he was suddenly addressed by Vsevolod, who said: " I am in great distress. My brother

* N. Kolossof, an Orthodox priest, states that at the end of 1910 Soloviev's confessor in the Sokolny Hospital made the following statement: " Soloviev told me that, some years previously, his last Orthodox confessor had refused him absolution for a point of dogma, but he did not tell me what it was." The dying man added that the refusal had been quite justifiable. There is no need to discuss this statement; it only shows that Soloviev, though he renounced his sins, retracted none of his theological conclusions.

has openly seceded to Catholicism, in order to receive the Eucharist, that our Church withholds
from him as a punishment." This conversation
was reported fifteen years after the events mentioned,
and only six months after the publication of Tolstoï's
account of them. If it had ended here, we might
think it strange, indiscreet and imprudent, but not
impossible, since the statement was correct. But
what follows seems almost incredible. Vsevolod
Soloviev is said to have added: " There is something
worse than that. I possess a letter in which my
brother is offered the priesthood; this proposal
emanated from Rome, but Vladimir's answer to it
was: ' I cannot accept less than a Cardinal's hat.' "
The narrator concludes by saying that Vsevolod
hurried away, after remarking seriously: " He will
be a Cardinal. Do not forget my words."

Undoubtedly both Vsevolod and M. Gnédine
were much excited on that day, and their emotion
may serve as an excuse for a story that is altogether
a mixture of memory and imagination. Gnédine's
general tone is by no means favourable to Soloviev,
and we cannot regard as probable either the alleged
offer from Rome or the answer to it. Those who
know anything of the usual procedure of the pontifical Court, and also those who ever came into
contact with Soloviev, will be amused at Vsevolod's
prophecy, and will feel gratitude to Gnédine for
having added: " This prophecy was not fulfilled.
Soloviev was a plain Uniate at the time of his death."

Nicolas Engelhardt made fun of these extremists
in a very gentle way in the *Novoïe Vremia* of August

21 (September 3), 1910. He says that the calumnies contained in these "yellow pages" and diocesan Bulletins will not sully the fame of one who has become more than a Bishop in Russia, since he is for us " a kind of Pope in the universal domain of intellect and thought." Profound thinkers, like Pertsov, could not be astonished if Soloviev, in the honesty of his soul, brought his practice and his faith into agreement. Both in action and in delay, he listened only to the voice of his own conscience, and no selfish arguments or human interests could influence him. Every detail in his conduct was inspired by the one wish to give honour to God, by bringing souls to Him through Christ. In his *Counterfeits of Christianity* he writes: " I am not founding a philosophical school of my own. But as I see the spread of deformities hostile to Christianity, I consider it my duty to reveal, in the fundamental idea of the Kingdom of God, what ought to constitute the fulness of human life, individual, social, and political—that life which Christ has destined to be perfectly united to the Godhead, through the agency of the living Church."

In a Russian work begun about the year 1882, Soloviev shows by what principles he was guided throughout the rest of his life. *The Religious Foundations*, or, according to the third edition, *The Spiritual Foundations of Life*, reveals to some extent the depth of his soul, and a résumé of this work will form a suitable conclusion to our study of Soloviev's character.   In it we shall find an answer to various questions that the reader no doubt feels inclined to ask—viz., With what intentions did he direct all his activity to the speculative and practical mastery of integral philosophy? How did he succeed in utilizing all his intellectual, moral and religious resources in such a wonderful manner, so as to bring them into perfect harmony? By what method did he develop himself in such a remarkable degree?

The preface begins with a clear statement: "Reason and conscience show us that our mortal life is bad and inconsistent." Instead of accepting pessimism, as his teachers had done, Soloviev, being then twenty-nine years of age, adds: "Reason and conscience alike call for an improvement of this life. To effect this, we must look beyond this life; and to the believer faith reveals this lever, that is superior to life, in religion." Thus the spiritual life assumes at least faith in God, and a conviction that "religion ought to regenerate and sanctify our life and unite it to the divine life. This is primarily the work of God, but it cannot be accomplished without our co-operation."

However, even as believers, "we generally live without God or in opposition to Him, heedless of other men and slaves of our lower nature. . . . Now true life requires us to adopt quite a contrary attitude—we should aim at voluntary submission to God, at mutual union with others and at the subjugation of nature. The first of these aims is realized in prayer, the second in active charity, and the third by controlling our lower

17

impulses and passions and so attaining to true liberty."

Prayer, sympathy with others, and control of the lower desires are for the individual the three fundamental elements in our relation to God, our Lord and Father, the Lord and Father also of our brethren, and the Ruler and End of all material creation.

The performance of our duties as individuals will naturally result in fidelity to the collective duties laid upon us as members of human society. "Every thought and every form of philosophy seeks unity. Now what gives the world, not only existence, but also true unity is the mighty, living, and personal power of God. His active unity is revealed to us in His works, but still more in the manifestation that unified God's majesty, human mind and corporal matter in the theandric person of Christ, in whom the fulness of the Divinity dwells in bodily form. . . . Without Christ we should not possess God's truth, and in the same way we should not know the truth of Christ if He were only a figure in history. It is not only in the past, but also in the present, and beyond the ordinary limits of our human life, that Christ in His living reality must be presented to us; and it is thus that we perceive Him in the Church. Those who fancy that they can dispense with any intermediary, and obtain personally a full and definite revelation of Christ, are *not ripe* for this revelation;* and mistake the phantoms of their own imagination for Christ.

* These two words are underlined by Soloviev.

We ought to seek the fulness of Christ, not in our individual sphere, but in that which is universal—viz., the Church."

There are, therefore, two parts in this work; both refer to the relations between man and God; the former deals with the individual, the latter with the social relations. The conclusion of the preface sums them up in a precept, underlined by Soloviev: . " Pray to God, do good to men, restrain your impulses; unite yourself inwardly to the theandric life of Christ; recognize His active presence in the Church, and make it your aim to bring His Spirit to bear upon every detail of natural, human life, in order that thus we may realize the theandric aim of our Creator, and heaven may be united with earth."

In the first part, before discussing the nature of prayer, Soloviev explains why man should believe in God. His spontaneous craving for immortality and justice reveal to him a Good proceeding neither from his individual reason nor from cosmic nature. He understands, then, that he has no right to live careless of this Good, and so his obligation to believe in God becomes plain. Yet this faith, superior to the assaults of our reason, must at the same time be given us by this Good, in such a way as not to violate our liberty.

When we realize our weakness, we feel the necessity of prayer. Whoever believes in the Good, knowing that he has nothing good in and by himself, must needs pray—*i.e.*, he seeks to unite himself with the essentially Good, and surrenders his own will—such spiritual sacrifice being prayer. " It is possible not to believe in God, and this is spiritual death, whereas to believe in oneself as the source of Good is absolute folly. True wisdom and the principle of moral perfection consist in believing in the divine source of all that is good, in believing in Him who is Good, praying to Him, and surrendering to Him our will in all things." Such is the teaching of the *Pater Noster*.

One of the most remarkable sections of the first part is a long and very beautiful discussion of the *Pater Noster*, with an analysis of the three temptations that successively assail a spiritual man, and that he will overcome only if accustomed to have recourse to God. We may select from it a few extracts.

The first temptation comes from the body, and suggests that a spiritual man is superior to right and wrong, and can no longer be stained with sin. When this temptation is conquered, it gives place to another: " After the spiritual man has prevailed over the temptation of the flesh, that of the spirit follows. ' You know the truth, and true life has begun within you. This is not given to all; others do not know the truth, as you see, and true life is strange to them. Although truth does not proceed from you (as the first temptation suggested), it nevertheless is yours. . . . To you it has been granted to receive true life, but not to others. . . . It must be that you were already better and higher than they were. And now ' . . ."

This temptation to self-satisfaction and self-love tends to substitute for an anxiety *to be* a desire *to appear ;* it has seduced men of worth and merit, changing them into founders of sects, heresiarchs, or promoters of national separatism. A truly spiritual man, who turns to God in prayer, when assailed by this temptation, will calmly say: " Truth is, in and of itself, eternal, infinite, and perfect. Our mind can never do more than participate in it. In truth there is no self-seeking. . . . If, then, I look upon truth as my private possession and make it an excuse for self-satisfaction and for preferring myself to others, I prove that I am not yet in the Truth." How could Truth ever dwell in the proud—*Veritas in eo non est*—when " it cannot be recognized except on a basis of humility and self-denial "?

The third temptation is ambition, which strives to raise our desires. " Lay claim," it says, " to power, in order to promote the reign of Good. Men know nothing of truth, so gain influence that you may bring them into subjection to God." A spiritual man will reply: " Yes, I ought to co-operate in the salvation of the world and in securing its practical submission to its divine principle. But it is false to say that, for this reason, I ought to strive to dominate the world. . . . If I truly desire God's work to be accomplished, in His name and according to His holy will, I have no right to *seek* any personal power, nor should I do anything with a view to acquiring it. I believe in God, and desire to do His work, I pray that His Kingdom may come, and I labour for this end according to the means given me, and not otherwise; for I know neither the secrets of His divine economy, nor the ways of His providence and the designs of His wisdom. I do not know what His designs are for me, nor for the world. My duty, therefore, is to promote the glory of God and the salvation of the world by the means bestowed upon me, and at the same time patiently to await their realization according to God's designs; thus, instead of aggravating the evil around me, I shall diminish it by my gentleness and kindness."

In this way the spiritual man resists every temptation by means of prayer. He perceives that in God's sight his interior life is only beginning. He is in God, and God is in him, but not all that is in him is of God. This truth, that God does not allow to be obscured for a man of prayer, destroys all the sophistries of self-love, because self-love is particularist and therefore opposed to the Good and Divine.

The practice of mercy and self-sacrifice will complete the work of prayer. The Eucharist is a perfect synthesis of absolute prayer, absolute mercy and absolute sacrifice.

It is plain, therefore, that religion cannot be a purely individual matter; it is necessarily social; and the whole human race collectively is called to union with God and His will. How can mankind be guided towards this ideal ?

Men, being unable to attain to this union by their own efforts, would not even conceive its greatness without a revelation; but, as it is, they can study an inimitable model of it in the Incarnate Word, in

His theandric work as Mediator, and above all in
His resurrection; but, if they find that Eucharistic
Communion is the most effectual means of developing the divine life in themselves, it is only through
the Church that they can be incorporated into it
The aim of the Church is to sanctify men by bringing
them into union with God. This sanctification
cannot be absolutely perfect and complete in any
of the visible members of the Church; yet it never
ceases to proceed from Christ and to diffuse itself
over the Church through the most holy and immaculate Virgin and the invisible Church of the saints.
Being thus sanctified by the Church, who, as a
Church, is not soiled by our sins, we ought to
acquiesce in losing our own souls for her sake, losing
the isolation of our human *ego*, in order to find those
souls again, enlarged by universal charity and raised
to a superhuman level by union with God. Such
detachment is natural to the simple, but it is more
difficult to a student, although he is the more bound
to practise it because, if he be a man of good will,
he receives more light on the truth. He will not
be surprised to discover progressive elucidations
of human origin attaching to the divine and unchanging dogma, culpable failures in duty on the
part of the divinely appointed hierarchy, and, in
the case of each of the seven sacraments, a whole
group of visible actions added to the essential
rite, in order to render it more comprehensible
to the faithful.

" Orthodoxy " has no right to condemn a Church
on the ground of growth in the manifestation of

the hierarchy, the truth and the sacraments. On
the contrary, such growth is commendable, provided
that it serves to throw more light upon the essential
characteristic of the true Church of Christ—viz.,
universality. Without such growth, the Church
would no longer be able to reveal herself, according
to God's will, as the *way*, in virtue of possessing
a visible hierarchy, the *truth*, through her unity
of infallibly promulgated dogma, and the *life*,
through her sacraments, that sanctify all who
receive them with good will. Now this threefold
manifestation is necessary, since the Church, being
founded by Christ in order to unite all mankind
with God, must inevitably be universal or Catholic,
both in time and space.

But this Catholic society that lives in the midst
of national societies and respects them, seems
likely to clash with the narrowness of nationalism
and the self-seeking of individuals. How can the
relations of local societies and their governments
be reconciled with the Church ? This subject is
discussed in the last chapter. " In a Christian
State, the sovereign power exists, but, far from being
a deification of human caprice, it is under a special
obligation to carry out the will of God. A representative of authority in a Christian State is not
only, like the pagan Cæsars, possessed of all the rights
to use it ; he is, above all, bound by all the obligations
arising from a peculiarly Christian attitude towards
the Church—*i.e.*, towards the action of God, on
earth." This truth will regulate the relations of
spiritual men with the civil power.

After this long explanation, Soloviev summed up his views in a magnificent conclusion, in which we can see what was the directing principle of all his activity, at least during the last fifteen years of his life. Its title is *The Example of Christ as the Guide of Conscience*, and it begins thus: " The supreme aim of individual and social morality is that Christ, in whom dwells the fulness of the Godhead in bodily form, shall be the model of all men in all things. Each of us can contribute towards the realization of this ideal, if we ourselves reproduce Christ in our personal and social life."

This, therefore, is the practical rule: " Before making any important decision, let us call up in our minds the image of Christ, and, concentrating our thoughts upon it, let us ask: Would He perform this action ? Or, in other words: Will He approve of it, nor not ? Will He bless me for this work, or not ?"

Soloviev adds: " I invite all to adopt this practice, for it never fails. In every case of doubt, whenever the possibility of a choice is offered you, remember Christ; think of Him as living, for He is so really, and confide to Him all your difficulties. . . . If men of good will, as individuals, or as members of society, or as leaders of their fellow-men and of nations, apply this principle, they will indeed have it in their power to point out to others the way to God, in the name of truth."

Soloviev was thirty when he wrote these forcible lines. Their emphatic character shows that he had already long been practising what he taught,

and to the end of his life he was careful to live, as
he advised others to live, in the presence and friendship of Christ. He sought and found Christ in His
universal Church, and he will still make Him known
to others. As Viscount de Vogüé remarked, Soloviev's face was enough to make one think of Christ,
his words taught men to love Him, and his example
should rouse many to follow Him.

On December 3, 1900, B. Spassovitch, writing
in the *Messager de l'Europe*, said: " All his contemporaries showed indifference to his chief practical
idea, the reunion of the Churches, and no one
followed him. However, if the life of nations is
defined by their religion, the importance of Roman
Catholicism must be admitted. If we divide Europe
into two groups, we shall undoubtedly find that
Catholic Europe stands on a higher moral and
spiritual level than do the anti-Catholic portions.
The conception of the world put forward by a man
like Dante Alighieri tends more directly towards
progress than does that of a man like Büchner;
St. Francis of Assisi ranks before Lassalle, and the
spirit of Joan of Arc cannot be compared with
Louise Michel."

Ten years later, on July 31 (August 13), 1910,
Petersov, writing in the *Novoïe Vremia*, drew attention to the great change due to Soloviev's
influence: " It seems," he says, " that he was still
writing only yesterday. He was a most ' contemporary ' writer, full of the spirit of the age. During
his life he appeared to have nothing to do with
time, but now we hear on all sides of societies,

committees, and associations bearing the name *Vladimir Soloviev ;* attention is now directed to the questions that absorbed all his energy, the mystical and religious value of life."

The question of questions is set to us by God, and He suggests the answer. God, as Soloviev used to say, gives us Himself through Christ, and gives us Christ through the Church. How happy we should be, amid all the distractions and cares that make up our days, to view all in the light of eternity, to know God is with us !

Printed in England.